PAY PULSE

PAY PULSE

It's all about Salary and Compensation for Economic Impacts

By

Avin Nisarg

Title:

PAY PULSE: It's All About Salary and Compensation for Economic Impacts

Author: Avin Nisarg

Edited and published by: Avin Nisarg (Self-published author)

Book design and cover design by: Avin Nisarg

Publisher's address: Kankavli, Maharashtra, India

E-mail: naturalavin@gmail.com

Edition: First (March 2024)

ISBN: 978 93 340 3888 0

"In Loving Memory of My Beloved Brothers,

Nitin [Aba] And Shailesh,

Who Fervently Championed

Social and Financial Equality

and Adamantly Opposed

Classism.

You Reside Forever in My Heart!"

"Resolutely Dedicated to

All Labourers, Workers and **Employees**

Around the World

Who are

Safeguarded by the Laws

but

Ignored by the Systems."

“This introductory, informative, and concise book is essential reading for every employee, worker, and labourer worldwide as it addresses their well-being, safety, security, and progress.”

- Avin Nisarg

TABLE OF CONTENTS

Preface

Dear Reader,

Welcome to
"Pay Pulse: It's all about Salary and Compensation for Economic Impacts."

As a self-published author passionate about empowering businesses to effectively manage their workforce, I embarked on this journey to share insights and strategies on compensation management. In today's dynamic business landscape, understanding the value of talent and how to compensate it appropriately is paramount. Through this book, I aim to provide entrepreneurs and business leaders with practical guidance and valuable information to navigate the complexities of compensation, ensuring a satisfied and motivated workforce.

Whether you're an HR professional, a business owner, a manager, or simply someone interested in understanding the intricate workings of employee rewards, you've picked up the right book.

This introductory and informative book is aimed at guiding and providing information on Salary and Compensation management to entrepreneurs, new business ventures, and newly formed organizations.

This introductory, informative, and concise book is essential reading for every employee, worker, and labourer worldwide as it addresses their well-being, safety, security, and progress.

In today's fast-paced and competitive landscape, compensation is not just about handing out paychecks. It's about strategically aligning incentives, benefits, and rewards to attract, retain, and motivate top talent while fostering a culture of fairness and equity within organizations.

This book is a comprehensive guide that delves into the multifaceted realm of compensation. From understanding the fundamentals of pay structures to navigating the complexities of legal and ethical considerations, each chapter offers valuable insights and practical strategies to help you navigate the ever-evolving landscape of employee rewards.

We'll embark on a journey through the historical evolution of salary systems, explore emerging trends in compensation practices, and examine case studies that illustrate real-world applications of compensation strategies. Whether you're a seasoned professional or new to the field, there's something in these pages for everyone.

As we dive into the intricacies of compensation, I encourage you to approach each chapter with an open mind and a thirst for knowledge. Let's explore the fascinating world of compensation together and uncover the keys to building a motivated, engaged, and high-performing workforce.

In an age marked by rapid technological change, evolving workforce dynamics, and unprecedented global challenges, the role of new entrepreneurs and emerging organizations in shaping the future of work and society is more critical than ever. It is with this understanding and a deep sense of responsibility that I embarked on writing this book, aimed at guiding these change makers through the multifaceted aspects of building and sustaining a successful enterprise.

My intention in authoring this book is rooted in a simple yet profound belief: that the well-being of society is intricately linked to how we manage our businesses, particularly in how we handle our manpower, funds, technology, and leverage government support. It's about crafting an ecosystem where businesses don't just thrive financially but also contribute positively to the lives of their employees and, by extension, to society at large.

As a guide for new entrepreneurs and organizations, this book is designed to demystify the complexities of setting up and running a business in today's dynamic environment. It navigates through the crucial aspects of managing manpower, aligning technology with business goals, utilizing government support effectively, and handling funds with foresight and responsibility. Each chapter is crafted with the dual aim of providing practical advice and encouraging progressive and sustainable changes in the business landscape.

The core philosophy of this book revolves around the symbiotic relationship between a business and its employees. A happy, motivated, and well-compensated workforce is not just an asset but the very engine that drives innovation and growth. Therefore, considerable emphasis is placed on creating salary systems and work environments that foster employee satisfaction and retention, recognizing that this is integral to long-term business success.

Moreover, this book addresses the need for businesses to be prepared and adaptable. In a world where change is the only constant, being equipped to pivot strategies, embrace technological advancements, and respond to societal needs is indispensable. From practical tips on navigating initial challenges to long-term strategies for sustainable growth, this book aims to be a comprehensive resource for those at the helm of steering their ventures toward success.

In essence, this book is more than just a manual for business management; it's a call to action for new entrepreneurs and organizations to lead with vision, empathy, and resilience. It's an invitation to be part of creating a future where businesses are not just successful in the conventional sense but are pillars of a progressive, equitable, and sustainable society.

As you turn these pages, I hope you find not just information and strategies, but also inspiration and confidence to embark on this challenging yet immensely rewarding journey of creating and nurturing a business that makes a difference.

Written by drawing upon publicly available information and enriched with my unique perspectives and experiences, this book offers a comprehensive and insightful exploration of its subject matter.

I invite you to enter into the pages of my book, where I share insights and perspectives aimed at igniting positive change. Your engagement and feedback are invaluable to me. Together, let's embark on a journey of discovery and discourse, where your suggestions and insights can further enrich the dialogue. By lending your voice to this conversation, you play a pivotal role in shaping a brighter future for our society. Join me in this endeavour, as together, we strive to make a lasting impact through the power of words and ideas.

Let us join hands to create a world where everyone has the chance to thrive. Together, we can champion initiatives that uplift the disadvantaged and empower communities. By collaborating and pooling our collective wisdom, we can forge pathways to prosperity that benefit all. Join me in this noble endeavour, as we work tirelessly to build a brighter, more equitable future for generations to come.

Thank you for choosing to join me on this journey. Let's begin.

With warm regards,

Avin Nisarg

Welcome to the path of impactful entrepreneurship!

Chapter 1

Introduction to Compensation

Welcome to the first chapter of the book, where we delve into the fundamental aspects of compensation. In today's dynamic and competitive business environment, understanding compensation is essential for both employers and employees. Compensation goes beyond just the paychecks — it encompasses various elements such as salaries, bonuses, benefits, and incentives that organizations offer to attract, retain, and motivate their workforce. This chapter serves as a comprehensive guide to help you grasp the importance of compensation in the workplace and set the stage for the chapters to follow. So, let's embark on this journey to unravel the intricacies of compensation together.

Definition and importance of compensation in the workplace.

Definition:

Compensation refers to the total package of rewards that employees receive in exchange for their work and services rendered to an organization. It goes beyond the basic salary and includes various elements such as wages, bonuses, benefits, incentives, and non-monetary perks. Compensation serves as a tangible expression of the value an organization places on its employees' contributions.

Importance:

1. Attracting and Retaining Talent

Competitive Advantage:

A well-structured compensation package can give an organization a competitive edge in the job market, attracting top talent.

Retention:

Fair and competitive compensation is crucial for retaining skilled employees and reducing turnover.

2. Motivation and Performance:

Incentive for Excellence:

Compensation, especially performance-based rewards, serves as a powerful motivator, encouraging employees to strive for excellence.

Productivity:

When employees perceive a direct link between their efforts and their compensation, they are more likely to be productive and committed to achieving organizational goals.

3. Employee Satisfaction and Morale:

Recognition and Value:

Adequate compensation demonstrates that the organization recognizes and values the contributions of its employees.

Job Satisfaction:

Employees who feel fairly compensated are generally more satisfied with their jobs and workplace.

4. Equity and Fairness:

Internal Equity:

Compensation ensures fairness within an organization by establishing consistent pay structures for similar roles.

External Equity:

Organizations must consider industry and market standards to maintain external fairness and competitiveness.

5. Employee Well-being:

Financial Stability:

Compensation contributes to employees' financial stability, addressing their basic needs and improving overall well-being.

Quality of Life:

Well-designed benefit packages, such as healthcare and retirement plans, enhance employees' quality of life.

6. Organizational Culture:

Alignment with Values:

Compensation practices should align with the values and culture of the organization, reinforcing a positive work environment.

Perception of Fairness:

Fair compensation fosters a positive perception of the organization, contributing to a healthy workplace culture.

7. Legal Compliance:

Adherence to Regulations:

Compensation systems must comply with local and national labour laws, ensuring legal obligations are met.

Avoidance of Litigation:

Fair compensation practices reduce the risk of legal issues and disputes related to wage and hour violations.

8. Employee Engagement and Loyalty:

Commitment:

Employees who feel fairly compensated are more likely to be engaged, committed, and loyal to the organization.

Reduced Turnover:

A comprehensive compensation strategy contributes to employee satisfaction, reducing the likelihood of talent attrition.

Compensation is a multifaceted concept that goes beyond monetary transactions. It plays a pivotal role in attracting, retaining, and motivating a skilled workforce while contributing to the overall success and sustainability of an organization. A strategic approach to compensation is essential for fostering a positive work environment and achieving long-term organizational goals.

Historical overview of salary systems and how they have evolved.

The evolution of salary systems is a complex and dynamic process that has been shaped by historical, economic, and social factors.

Here's a brief historical overview of salary systems and their evolution:

1. Barter System (Prehistoric to Ancient Times):

In the earliest human societies, people exchanged goods and services through barter, where direct trade occurred without a standardized medium of exchange.

Labour was often compensated with goods or necessities rather than a standardized form of currency.

2. Ancient Civilizations (3000 BCE - 476 CE):

With the emergence of complex societies like Mesopotamia, Egypt, Greece, and Rome, currencies such as silver, gold, and copper coins became more prevalent.

Labourers received wages in the form of coins or commodities, and payment often depended on the type of work performed.

3. Feudal System (9th to 15th Century):

During the medieval period, feudalism dominated Europe. Labourers, known as serfs, were tied to the land and received compensation in the form of protection, land, and a share of the harvest. Monetary wages were less common, and the system was based on a hierarchical structure with lords and vassals.

4. Guild System (12th to 17th Century):

Craftsmen and artisans formed guilds, which regulated wages and working conditions within specific trades.

Wages were often set by the guilds, and apprenticeship systems were established to ensure skill development.

5. Industrial Revolution (18th to 19th Century):

The shift from agrarian economies to industrialization brought about significant changes in salary systems.

Factory workers were paid wages in cash, marking a transition from the previous systems. However, working conditions were often harsh.

6. Taylorism and Scientific Management (Late 19th Century):

Frederick Taylor's scientific management principles introduced time-based payment systems, emphasizing efficiency and productivity.

Piece-rate systems and time-and-motion studies became popular, linking pay directly to output.

7. Rise of Labor Movements (Late 19th to Early 20th Century):

Labour unions gained strength, advocating for better working conditions and fair wages.

Collective bargaining led to the establishment of minimum wage standards and standardized working hours.

8. Post-World War II Era (Mid-20th Century):

The mid-20th century saw the rise of social welfare systems and increased government intervention in labour markets.

Salary structures became more standardized, with the introduction of benefits such as health insurance and retirement plans.

9. Globalization and Information Age (Late 20th Century to Present):

The late 20th century witnessed globalization, impacting salary differentials across regions.

The rise of the information age led to increased demand for knowledge workers, influencing compensation structures based on skills and expertise.

10. Technology and Flexible Compensation (21st Century):

Advancements in technology have facilitated the use of digital platforms for remote work and freelancing, impacting traditional salary structures.

Flexible compensation packages, including stock options, bonuses, and other non-monetary benefits, have become more prevalent.

The evolution of salary systems reflects the broader shifts in economic, social, and technological landscapes, with ongoing adaptations to meet the changing needs of the workforce and the economy.

What compensation is, encompassing not just salary but also benefits and incentives.

Compensation refers to the total package of rewards that employees receive in exchange for their work and contributions to an organization. It goes beyond the simple concept of salary and includes various components such as benefits and incentives.

Here's a breakdown of the different elements that make up compensation:

1. Base Salary:

The fixed amount of money that an employee receives regularly, typically on a monthly or bi-weekly basis.

It is the core component of compensation and serves as the foundation for an individual's total earnings.

2. Benefits:

Health Insurance:

Coverage for medical, dental, and sometimes vision expenses, either partially or fully funded by the employer.

Retirement Plans:

Contributions to pension funds, 401(k) plans, or other retirement savings programs to help employees plan for their future.

Life Insurance:

Coverage that provides financial protection to the employee's beneficiaries in the event of their death.

Paid Time Off (PTO):

Vacation days, sick leave, and holidays that allow employees to take time away from work with pay.

Flexible Spending Accounts (FSAs) or Health Savings Accounts (HSAs):

Pre-tax accounts that employees can use to cover eligible medical expenses.

3. Incentives:

Bonuses:

Additional payments made to employees as a reward for achieving specific performance targets or goals.

Profit Sharing:

A program where employees receive a share of the company's profits, promoting a sense of ownership and alignment of interests.

Commission:

A variable payment based on sales or other performance metrics, common in industries like sales and retail.

Stock Options or Equity Grants:

Providing employees with the opportunity to buy company stock at a predetermined price, aligning their interests with the organization's success.

4. Non-Monetary Perks:

Flexible Work Arrangements:

Offering options such as remote work, flexible hours, or compressed workweeks to enhance work-life balance.

Professional Development Opportunities:

Investing in training, education, and skill development to help employees grow in their careers.

Employee Assistance Programs (EAPs):

Services that support employees' well-being, including counselling, mental health resources, and stress management.

5. Performance Recognition:

Recognition Programs:

Acknowledging and rewarding exceptional performance through formal or informal recognition programs.

Promotions and Advancement Opportunities:

Providing opportunities for career growth and progression based on performance and achievements.

A comprehensive compensation strategy takes into account all these elements, aiming to attract, motivate, and retain talented employees. It is designed not only to meet the financial needs of employees but also to create a positive and supportive work environment that contributes to overall job satisfaction and employee engagement. Effective compensation packages are often tailored to the organization's industry, culture, and the specific needs and expectations of its workforce.

Why a well-designed compensation system is crucial for attracting and retaining talent.

A well-designed compensation system plays a crucial role in attracting and retaining talent for several reasons:

1. Competitive Advantage:

In a competitive job market, organizations must offer competitive salaries and benefits to attract top talent. A well designed compensation system ensures that the organization remains competitive within its industry and geographic location.

2. Talent Attraction:

Prospective employees often evaluate job opportunities based on the compensation package offered. A competitive salary, along with attractive benefits and incentives, serves as a powerful magnet for attracting skilled and experienced professionals.

3. Retention of High-Performers:

An effective compensation system goes beyond initial attraction; it also focuses on retaining high-performing employees. Recognizing and rewarding exceptional performance through bonuses, incentives, and advancement opportunities helps keep valuable talent within the organization.

4. Motivation and Productivity:

Well-designed compensation systems include performance-based incentives that motivate employees to perform at their best. When employees see a direct link between their efforts and financial rewards, they are likely to be more motivated and productive.

5. Employee Satisfaction and Engagement:

Compensation is a significant factor influencing overall job satisfaction. When employees feel fairly compensated for their skills and contributions, they are more likely to be satisfied with their jobs and engaged in their work.

6. Market Perception:

A competitive compensation system positively impacts the organization's reputation in the job market. A reputation for offering attractive compensation packages can make the organization an employer of choice, drawing more interest from potential candidates.

7. Reduction of Turnover Costs:

High turnover can be costly for organizations in terms of recruitment, onboarding, and training expenses. A well-designed compensation system that aligns with employee needs reduces the likelihood of turnover, saving the organization money and preserving institutional knowledge.

8. Talent Development and Succession Planning:

Compensation systems that include opportunities for professional development and career advancement contribute to talent development. Employees are more likely to stay with an organization that invests in their growth and provides a clear path for advancement.

9. Alignment with Organizational Goals:

A well-designed compensation system aligns individual and team performance with the overall goals of the organization.

This alignment ensures that employees are focused on activities that contribute to the organization's success.

10. Diversity and Inclusion:

A thoughtful compensation system can support diversity and inclusion efforts by ensuring fair and equitable pay for all employees. Addressing pay gaps and promoting transparency in compensation practices helps create an inclusive workplace culture.

Conclusion

A well-designed compensation system is a strategic tool for attracting, motivating, and retaining talent. It not only meets the financial needs of employees but also contributes to a positive organizational culture, employee satisfaction, and overall business success. Organizations that prioritize and invest in their compensation strategies are better positioned to build a talented and dedicated workforce.

"Employees are the wheels of the business, and they must run smoothly; similarly, salary and compensation are the fuel of the business, which must be pure and unadulterated."

Chapter 2

Types of Compensation

Welcome to the second chapter of the book, where we explore the diverse landscape of compensation strategies. Compensation comes in many forms, ranging from traditional salary and wages to innovative perks and incentives. Understanding the various types of compensation is crucial for organizations to design effective reward systems that align with their business objectives and meet the diverse needs of their workforce. In this chapter, we will delve into the intricacies of different compensation models, including direct and indirect compensation, fixed and variable pay structures, as well as non-monetary benefits. By the end of this chapter, you will have a comprehensive understanding of the different compensation options available and their implications for both employers and employees.

So, let's dive into the world of compensation and explore the myriad ways organizations reward their employees for their contributions.

I) Fixed salary and hourly wages:

Fixed salaries and hourly wages are two common methods of compensating employees, each with its own set of advantages and disadvantages. Details and the differences between fixed salaries and hourly wages.

Here's an overview of the differences between fixed salaries and hourly wages:

A) Fixed Salaries:

1. Definition:

A fixed salary is a predetermined, regular payment that employees receive consistently, regardless of the number of hours worked.

2. Advantages:

Stability:

Employees can depend on a stable income, making it easier to budget and plan personal finances.

Predictability:

Employers can forecast labour costs more accurately, as the salary remains constant regardless of variations in working hours.

Professionalism:

Salaried positions often come with a sense of professional status, indicating a certain level of responsibility and commitment.

3. Disadvantages:

Overtime Issues:

Salaried employees may not receive additional pay for working overtime, which can lead to longer working hours without additional compensation.

Lack of Flexibility:

Fixed salaries may not account for variations in workload or periods of increased effort.

B) Hourly Wages:

1. Definition:

Hourly wages involve compensating employees based on the number of hours they work. The payment is typically calculated by multiplying the hourly rate by the number of hours worked.

2. Advantages:

Fair Compensation for Hours Worked:
Hourly wages provide direct compensation for the actual time spent working, including overtime pay for hours beyond the standard workweek.

Flexibility:
Employers can adjust labour costs based on fluctuating workloads by hiring employees on an hourly basis.

Motivation for Productivity:
Knowing that additional hours result in increased pay can motivate employees to be more productive.

3. Disadvantages:

Income Variability:
Hourly workers may experience income variability due to fluctuations in work hours, making it challenging to budget consistently.

Administrative Challenges:
Managing hourly employees may require more detailed timekeeping and payroll administration.

Potential for Inconsistency:
Hourly workers might experience inconsistencies in work hours, making it difficult to maintain a work-life balance.

Considerations for Employers:

1. Nature of Work:

Jobs with consistent work hours and responsibilities may be well-suited for salaried positions, while roles with varying workloads or part-time arrangements may be more appropriate for hourly wages.

2. Employment Laws:

Employment laws and regulations may influence the choice between salaries and hourly wages. For example, minimum wage laws and overtime regulations often apply differently to salaried and hourly workers.

3. Employee Preferences:

Some employees may prefer the stability of a fixed salary, while others may appreciate the flexibility and direct correlation between effort and pay offered by hourly wages.

4. Industry Norms:

Practices within specific industries can also influence the choice between fixed salaries and hourly wages. For example, certain professions traditionally have salaried positions, while others rely more heavily on hourly compensation.

The choice between fixed salaries and hourly wages depends on various factors, including the nature of the work, employee preferences, and industry norms. Employers should carefully consider these factors to establish a compensation structure that aligns with both organizational needs and the expectations of their workforce.

II) Bonuses and Incentives:

Discussion on various bonus structures and incentive programs, linking them to performance metrics.

Various bonus structures and incentive programs are key tools used by organizations to motivate employees and align their efforts with company objectives. These programs are typically tied to specific performance metrics to ensure that the incentives offered directly reflect the contributions and achievements of employees.

Here's an overview of common bonus structures and incentive programs, along with their associated performance metrics:

1. Individual Performance Bonuses:

Structure:
These bonuses are awarded based on an individual's performance against predefined objectives.

Performance Metrics:
Often linked to individual targets such as sales goals, project completion, quality of work, or achievement of specific milestones.

Example:
A salesperson might receive a bonus for exceeding their sales targets for the quarter.

2. Team-Based Bonuses:

Structure:
Bonuses are awarded based on the performance of a team or department.

Performance Metrics:
Common metrics include team sales targets, project delivery within budget and timeline, team productivity levels, or collective quality metrics.

Example:
A project team might receive a bonus for completing a major project ahead of schedule and under budget.

3. Profit-Sharing Plans:

Structure:
Employees receive a share of the company's profits.

Performance Metrics:
Typically linked to the overall profitability of the company.

Example:
An annual bonus based on a percentage of the profits the company earned in the fiscal year.

4. Gainsharing Programs:

Structure:
Similar to profit-sharing, but focused more on operational improvements.

Performance Metrics:
Often linked to cost-saving measures, efficiency improvements, or productivity increases.

Example:
Employees in a manufacturing plant might receive bonuses for reducing waste and increasing output.

5. Stock Options and Equity-Based Incentives:

Structure:
Employees receive options to buy company stock at a favourable price, or shares of company stock directly.

Performance Metrics:
Usually linked to long-term company performance metrics, such as stock price appreciation or total shareholder return.

Example:
Executives receiving stock options that vest over several years, encouraging long-term commitment to the company.

6. Commission-Based Incentives:

Structure:
Primarily used in sales, commissions are a type of incentive that directly relates to the amount of sales generated.

Performance Metrics:
Typically based on the volume or value of sales made.

Example:

A salesperson receives a certain percentage of the value of the sales they make.

7. Non-Financial Recognition Programs:

Structure:
These programs reward employees with non-monetary incentives, such as awards, certificates, or public acknowledgement.

Performance Metrics:
This can be linked to various qualitative metrics like customer satisfaction scores, teamwork, leadership qualities, or innovative ideas.

Example:
Employee of the Month awards based on peer nominations for outstanding contribution or teamwork.

8. Goal-Based Incentives:

Structure:
Employees receive bonuses for meeting or exceeding specific operational goals.

Performance Metrics:
Tied to specific, measurable goals such as reducing operational costs, improving customer satisfaction scores, or meeting project deadlines.

Example:
IT staff receiving a bonus for successfully implementing a new software system ahead of the deadline.

9. Retention Bonuses:

Structure:
Aimed at retaining key employees, especially during periods of transition or uncertainty.

Performance Metrics:

Often linked to the length of service or staying with the company through a critical period.

Example:
Employees offered a bonus to stay with the company for a certain period following a merger or acquisition.

Implementation Considerations:

1. Alignment with Business Goals:

Incentive programs should align with the overall strategy and goals of the business.

2. Transparency and Fairness:

Clear communication of how bonuses are calculated and distributed is crucial for employee acceptance and motivation.

3. Flexibility:

Programs should be reviewed and adjusted regularly to remain relevant and effective.

4. Legal and Ethical Compliance:

Ensure that all incentive programs comply with labour laws and ethical standards.

Well-designed bonus structures and incentive programs, when tied to appropriate performance metrics, can effectively motivate employees, drive performance, and contribute to the achievement of organizational goals.

III) Benefits and Perks:

Some common employee benefits and perks, such as healthcare, retirement plans, and stock options.

Employee benefits and perks are essential components of a comprehensive compensation package that organizations offer to attract, retain, and motivate their workforce. These benefits go beyond the basic salary and contribute to employees' overall well-being and job satisfaction.

Here are some common employee benefits and perks:

1. Healthcare Benefits:

Medical Insurance:
Coverage for medical expenses, including doctor visits, hospital stays, prescription medications, and preventive care.

Dental Insurance:
Coverage for dental services, including cleanings, fillings, and orthodontic treatment.

Vision Insurance:
Coverage for eye care services, including eye exams, glasses, and contact lenses.

2. Retirement Plans:

i) 401 (k) Plans:

Employer-sponsored retirement savings plans that allow employees to contribute a portion of their salary on a pre-tax basis, often with employer-matching contributions.

What is a 401(k) plan in the salary system, here is the explanation with an example

A 401(k) plan is a type of retirement savings account provided by employers to their employees in the United States. It allows employees to contribute a portion of their pre-tax earnings into a retirement account, which is then invested in various financial instruments such as stocks, bonds, and mutual funds.

Here's how a 401(k) plan typically works:

a) Employee Contributions:

Employees can choose to contribute a percentage of their salary, up to a certain limit set by the Internal Revenue Service (IRS), into their 401(k) account. These contributions are deducted directly from their paychecks before taxes are applied, reducing their taxable income for the year.

b) Employer Contributions:

Some employers offer matching contributions to their employees' 401(k) accounts as part of their benefits package. For example, an employer might match 50 % of an employee's contributions, up to a certain percentage of their salary. This is essentially free money added to the employee's retirement savings.

c) Tax Benefits:

The contributions made by employees to their 401(k) accounts are tax-deferred, meaning they are not subject to income tax until they are withdrawn during retirement. This allows the investments in the account to grow tax-free over time, potentially leading to higher returns compared to taxable accounts.

d) Investment Options:

Employees have the opportunity to choose from a variety of investment options offered within their 401(k) plan, typically including a range of mutual funds, index funds, and target-date funds. They can adjust their investment allocations based on their risk tolerance and retirement goals.

e) Vesting:

Employer contributions to a 401(k) plan may be subject to a vesting schedule, which determines when employees become fully entitled to those contributions. Vesting schedules can vary depending on the employer's policy but typically range from immediate vesting to a graded schedule over a certain number of years.

Example:

Let's say John works for Company XYZ, which offers a 401(k) plan. John decides to contribute 5 % of his $ 50,000 annual salaries to his 401(k) account. Company XYZ also offers a 50 % match on employee contributions, up to 6 % of their salary.

John's annual contribution: 5% of $ 50,000 = $ 2,500

Company XYZ's matching contribution: 50 % of $ 2,500 = $1,250

In this scenario, John contributes $ 2,500 to his 401(k) account, and Company XYZ adds $1,250 as a matching contribution. Therefore, John's total annual contribution to his 401(k) account is $ 3,750.

Is the 401(k) plan of the US the same as the Provident Fund scheme of India?

While both the 401(k) plan in the United States and the Provident Fund scheme in India are retirement savings plans, they have some key differences:

a) Structure:

401(k) Plan:
The 401(k) plan is a defined contribution plan, where employees contribute a portion of their pre-tax income to their retirement account. Employers may also offer matching contributions. The account balance depends on the contributions made and the investment performance.

Provident Fund Scheme:
The Provident Fund scheme in India includes both the Employee Provident Fund (EPF) and the Public Provident Fund (PPF). It is a mandatory retirement savings scheme for employees, with contributions from both the employer and

the employee. The contributions are invested in fixed-income instruments and earn a guaranteed rate of return.

b) Management:

401(k) Plan:
Employees typically have control over how their contributions are invested, with a range of investment options offered by the plan.

Provident Fund Scheme:
The investments in the Provident Fund scheme are managed by government-appointed authorities, with a focus on low-risk fixed-income instruments.

c) Withdrawals:

401(k) Plan:
Withdrawals from a 401(k) account are generally allowed after reaching the age of 59½, although early withdrawals may be subject to penalties.

Provident Fund Scheme:
Withdrawals from the Provident Fund scheme are allowed under certain circumstances, such as retirement, resignation, or financial emergencies. However, there may be restrictions and tax implications depending on the reason for withdrawal.

d) Tax Treatment:

401(k) Plan:
Contributions to a traditional 401(k) plan are made on a pre-tax basis, reducing taxable income in the year of contribution.

Withdrawals during retirement are subject to income tax.

Provident Fund Scheme:
Contributions to the Provident Fund scheme qualify for tax deductions under Section 80C of the Income Tax Act in India. Interest earned on contributions is tax-exempt, and withdrawals may be tax-free under certain conditions.

Overall, while both the 401(k) plan in the US and the Provident Fund scheme in India serve as retirement savings vehicles, they have different structures, management approaches, and tax treatments.

ii) Pension Plans:

Traditional defined benefit plans that provide a specific monthly benefit upon retirement based on factors like salary and years of service.

3. Stock Options and Equity:

Stock Options:
The right to purchase company stock at a predetermined price.

Restricted Stock Units (RSUs):
Actual shares of company stock granted to employees, typically vesting over a specified period.

4. Paid Time Off (PTO):

Vacation Days:
Paid time off for leisure, travel, or personal activities.

Sick Leave:
Paid time off for illness or medical appointments.

Holidays:
Paid days off for recognized public holidays.

5. Insurance Benefits:

Life Insurance:
Coverage that provides a lump-sum payment to beneficiaries in the event of the employee's death.

Disability Insurance:

Income protection in the event of a disability that prevents an employee from working.

6. Flexible Spending Accounts (FSAs) and Health Savings Accounts (HSAs):

FSAs:
Pre-tax accounts that allow employees to set aside money for eligible medical expenses.

HSAs:
Tax-advantaged accounts for individuals with high-deductible health plans, allowing them to save for qualified medical expenses.

7. Wellness Programs:

Fitness Memberships:
Subsidized or discounted memberships to gyms or fitness classes.

Health Screenings:
Programs that offer health assessments, screenings, and preventive measures.

8. Professional Development:

Training and Development Opportunities:
Programs that support employees in acquiring new skills and advancing their careers.

Educational Assistance:
Reimbursement or assistance for tuition and education-related expenses.

9. Childcare Assistance:

Childcare Subsidies:
Financial support for employees with children to help cover the costs of childcare.

On-Site Childcare Facilities:
Some organizations provide on-site childcare facilities for employees' convenience.

10. Transportation Benefits:

Commute Subsidies:
Financial assistance or subsidies for commuting expenses.

Company Vehicles or Car Allowances:
Some roles may include the provision of company cars or allowances for personal vehicle use.

11. Remote Work and Flexible Schedules:

Telecommuting Options:
The ability to work remotely, either partially or full-time.

Flexible Work Hours:
Allows employees to set their working hours within certain limits.

12. Employee Assistance Programs (EAPs):

Counselling Services:
Confidential counselling services to assist employees with personal or work-related challenges.

Well-being Resources:
Access to resources and information on mental health, stress management, and work-life balance.

13. Recognition and Rewards Programs:

Employee Recognition:
Programs that acknowledge and reward outstanding performance.

Incentive Programs:

Bonuses or rewards for achieving specific performance targets.

Considerations for Employers:

1. Tailoring Benefits Packages:

Understanding the diverse needs of the workforce and tailoring benefits packages to address those needs.

2. Communication:

Transparent communication about the available benefits to ensure employees are aware of and can make the most of them.

3. Legal Compliance:

Ensuring that all benefit programs comply with relevant employment laws and regulations.

Conclusion

A well-designed and competitive benefits package contributes to employee satisfaction, engagement, and retention, ultimately enhancing the overall success of the organization.

"Salaries are not just expenses; they're investments in talent and dedication."

Chapter 3

Understanding Pay Structures

In this chapter, we embark on a journey to unravel the complexities of pay structures within organizations. Pay structures form the foundation of compensation systems, determining how employees are rewarded for their contributions. From traditional hierarchical structures to modern competency-based frameworks, pay structures come in various forms, each with its own advantages and challenges. We will explore the key components of pay structures, including salary bands, grade levels, and pay ranges, and discuss the factors that influence their design and implementation. By gaining a deeper understanding of pay structures, organizations can ensure fairness, transparency, and alignment with their business objectives. Join us as we delve into the intricacies of pay structures and uncover the principles that underpin effective compensation management.

How organizations determine salary levels:

Determining salary levels in organizations involves a strategic and systematic process that takes into account various factors to ensure fairness, competitiveness, and alignment with the organization's goals.

Here's a detailed overview of how organizations typically determine salary levels:

1. Market Research and Benchmarking:

Organizations often start by conducting market research to understand industry salary trends and benchmarks. This involves comparing salaries for similar roles in comparable organizations within the same geographical region or industry.

2. Job Analysis and Evaluation:

Conducting a thorough job analysis to understand the responsibilities, requirements, and qualifications for each position. Job evaluation methods, such as point-factor systems, may be used to assign a relative value to each job within the organization.

3. Internal Equity:

Ensuring internal equity by comparing the value of different jobs within the organization. This involves establishing a fair and consistent pay structure based on the relative worth of each position in terms of skills, responsibilities, and contribution to organizational objectives.

4. Compensation Surveys:

Participating in or purchasing compensation surveys to gather data on salary levels in the industry. These surveys provide information on market trends, salary ranges, and benefits, helping organizations make informed decisions about their compensation packages.

5. Legal and Regulatory Compliance:

Adhering to legal and regulatory requirements related to compensation, such as minimum wage laws, equal pay regulations, and other labour laws. Ensuring compliance helps prevent legal issues and promotes fairness in pay practices.

6. Organizational Budget and Financial Health:

Considering the organization's financial health and budget constraints when determining salary levels. Budgetary limitations may influence the ability to offer competitive salaries or implement certain benefits.

7. Performance Management:

Linking salary levels to individual and overall performance. High-performing employees may receive higher salary increases or bonuses, aligning compensation with contributions to organizational success.

8. Skill and Experience:

Taking into account the skills, qualifications, and experience required for a particular role. Employees with specialized skills or extensive experience may command higher salary levels.

9. Geographic Location:

Considering the cost of living and market competitiveness in different geographic locations. Salaries may be adjusted based on regional variations to attract and retain talent in specific areas.

10. Employee Negotiation and Bargaining:

In cases where collective bargaining agreements exist or during individual negotiations, organizations may consider employee requests and negotiate salary levels based on factors such as experience, education, and market conditions.

11. Benefits and Perks:

Including benefits and perks as part of the overall compensation package. These may include health insurance, retirement plans, stock options, bonuses, and other non-monetary benefits that contribute to the total compensation value.

12. Retention Strategies:

Considering salary levels as part of a broader retention strategy. Offering competitive salaries helps retain key talent and reduces turnover costs.

13. Communication and Transparency:

Communicating clearly with employees about the factors influencing salary levels and the organization's compensation philosophy. Transparency fosters trust and understanding among employees.

14. Regular Review and Adjustment:

Regularly reviewing and adjusting salary levels to remain competitive in the market and to account for changes in job responsibilities, market conditions, or the organization's strategic priorities.

Considerations for Small and Large Organizations:

1. Flexibility:

Smaller organizations may need to be more flexible and creative in their compensation strategies, while larger organizations may have more resources for complex compensation structures.

2. Industry Dynamics:

Salary determination should consider industry-specific factors, such as the demand for certain skills, competition for talent, and industry-specific pay practices.

Determining salary levels is a multifaceted process that requires a combination of market analysis, internal equity considerations, legal compliance, and strategic alignment with organizational goals. An effective and fair compensation strategy contributes to employee satisfaction, retention, and overall organizational success.

Different Pay Structures:

Explanation of flat, tiered, and commission-based pay structures. Understanding different pay structures is crucial for both employers and employees as they offer various incentives and align differently with organizational goals and employee performance. Here are explanations of flat, tiered, and commission-based pay structures, along with examples:

1. Flat Pay Structure:

A flat pay structure, often referred to as "single-rate pay," means employees are paid a fixed salary or hourly rate regardless of their performance or seniority. This structure is simple and straightforward, promoting transparency and equality but may not effectively incentivize high performance.

Example:

Call Centre Operator:

A call centre may pay its operators a flat rate of $15 per hour, irrespective of the number of calls handled or the length of their service. Whether an employee handles 30 calls or 50 calls in a shift, their pay remains the same.

Advantages:

Simplified payroll processing.

Easy to understand and transparent.

Ensures equality among employees performing the same role.

Disadvantages:

Limited motivation for employees to exceed expectations.

It may not attract high-performers looking for performance-based incentives.

Less flexibility to reward exceptional work or seniority.

2. Tiered Pay Structure:

In a tiered pay structure, employees are paid based on predefined levels or tiers that typically reflect their skill level, experience, or performance. This structure can motivate employees to improve their performance or skills to move up to a higher pay tier.

Example:

Software Developer Tiers:

A tech company might have different salary tiers for software developers: Junior Developer, Senior Developer, and Lead Developer. As employees gain experience and skills, they can progress to a higher tier with a corresponding salary increase.

Advantages:

Encourages skill development and career progression.

Rewards experience and performance, potentially improving retention.

More tailored to individual employee contributions than a flat structure.

Disadvantages:

Potentially more complex to administer.

Risk of creating competition or resentment among employees.

It may require regular assessment to determine tier placement.

3. Commission-Based Pay Structure:

Commission-based pay structures are predominantly performance-oriented, where employees earn based on the value or volume of sales they make or deals they close. This structure is common in sales-oriented roles and can highly incentivize performance.

Example:

Real Estate Agent:

A real estate agent might earn a 3 % commission on the sale price of each property they sell. If they sell a house priced at $ 500,000, they earn $15,000. Their total earnings are directly tied to how many properties they sell and at what price.

Advantages:

Highly incentivizes employees to perform better.

Directly ties compensation to measurable results.

Can attract highly motivated and competitive individuals.

Disadvantages:

Earnings can be unpredictable, leading to financial instability for employees.

It may not encourage teamwork, focusing solely on individual performance.

Can create high-pressure work environments.

Considerations for Employers:

1. Nature of the Job:

Choose a pay structure that aligns with the nature of the job and the business model.

2. Employee Motivation:

Consider what motivates the workforce – stability (flat pay), career progression (tiered pay), or high-earning potential (commission-based).

3. Market Standards:

Be aware of common pay structures in the industry to remain competitive.

The choice of pay structure should align with the organization's goals, the nature of the job, and what motivates its employees. Each structure has its unique set of advantages and challenges, impacting employee satisfaction and performance.

How organizations decide on the most suitable structure for their needs:

Deciding on the most suitable pay structure is a critical decision for organizations and involves considering factors such as the nature of the work, industry practices, organizational culture, and the desired outcomes. Here are some global examples that highlight how organizations decide on suitable pay structures:

1. Flat Pay Structure:

Example:
Basecamp (formerly 37signals)

Rationale:
Basecamp, a project management software company, is known for its flat organizational structure and flat pay model. They believe in simplicity and transparency, paying everyone the same base salary for a particular role, regardless of seniority or experience. This approach aligns with their philosophy of fostering collaboration and avoiding unnecessary hierarchy.

2. Tiered Pay Structure:

Example:

Google

Rationale:

Google has a tiered pay structure based on job roles and levels. Employees can progress through different levels, each with a corresponding pay band. This approach aligns with Google's emphasis on recognizing and rewarding talent and contributions. The tiered structure motivates employees to advance in their careers within the organization.

3. Commission-Based Pay Structure:

Example:

Salesforce

Rationale:
Salesforce, a cloud-based software company, is known for its commission-based pay structure for its sales team. Sales representatives earn commissions based on the value of the deals they close. This approach aligns with the sales-driven nature of the business, providing strong incentives for sales representatives to drive revenue.

4. Performance-Based Pay Structure:

Example:
General Electric (GE)

Rationale:
General Electric is known for its performance-based pay structure, where a significant portion of executive compensation is tied to performance metrics. This approach aligns with GE's focus on accountability and performance-driven results. Executives' bonuses and stock options are often tied to achieving specific financial and operational goals.

5. Skill and Competency-Based Pay Structure:

Example:
IBM

Rationale:
IBM has a competency-based pay structure, emphasizing skill development and expertise. Employees are compensated based on their skills, certifications, and competencies relevant to their roles. This approach aligns with IBM's emphasis on innovation and continuous learning.

6. Profit-Sharing and Employee Ownership:

Example:
The John Lewis Partnership (UK)

Rationale:
The John Lewis Partnership is an employee-owned retail company in the UK. Employees, known as "Partners," receive a share of the company's annual profits. This structure aligns with the company's commitment to shared ownership and a sense of shared responsibility among employees.

Let's Explore Performance-Based Compensation in Detail

Linking pay to performance:

The concept of performance-based pay, including merit increases, performance bonuses, and recognition programs. Performance-based pay, also known as incentive pay or pay-for-performance, is a compensation strategy where employees' compensation is directly related to their performance and productivity. This concept is designed to motivate employees, increase efficiency, and align employees' objectives with the company's goals. Performance-based pay can take several forms, including merit increases, performance bonuses, and recognition programs.

Let's explore each of these:

1. Merit Increases:

Definition:
Merit increases are pay raises awarded to employees based on their job performance. These are often annual adjustments to base pay.

Evaluation:
Performance is typically evaluated using a formal appraisal process, considering factors like achievement of targets, quality of work, and overall contribution to the company.

Impact:
Merit increases are meant to reward high-performing employees and encourage continued excellence. They can also help in retaining top talent.

2. Performance Bonuses:

Definition:
Performance bonuses are one-time payments given for achieving specific performance targets or completing a project. These are not added to the base salary.

Criteria:
Bonuses are usually tied to individual, team, or company performance metrics such as sales targets, project completion, or profitability.

Flexibility:
This form of compensation allows companies to reward achievements without committing to a permanent pay increase.

3. Recognition Programs:

Definition:
Recognition programs are designed to acknowledge and reward employees for exceptional work or contributions that may not be directly tied to quantifiable targets.

Types:
This can include Employee of the Month awards, service awards, or informal recognition such as public acknowledgement in meetings.

Purpose:

These programs aim to boost morale and create a positive work environment. They are also important for employee engagement and motivation.

Advantages of Performance-Based Pay:

1. Motivation and Productivity:

Tying compensation to performance can motivate employees to work harder and smarter to achieve their goals.

2. Alignment of Goals:

Helps in aligning employees' objectives with organizational goals.

3. Talent Attraction and Retention:

Attractive for high-performers who are confident in their abilities to meet and exceed performance standards.

4. Flexible Compensation Costs:

Allows companies to manage compensation costs in alignment with business performance.

Challenges and Considerations:

1. Subjectivity in Evaluation:

Performance appraisals can sometimes be subjective, leading to perceptions of unfairness.

2. Short-Term Focus:

Employees might focus more on short-term achievements at the expense of long-term goals.

3. Stress and Competition:

This can create excessive competition and stress among employees.

4. Dependency on Clear Metrics:

The success of a performance-based system depends on clear, achievable, and fair performance metrics.

Best Practices:

1. Clear Communication:

Clearly define performance metrics and how they are linked to compensation.

2. Regular Feedback:

Provide regular feedback, not just annual reviews, to help employees understand expectations and improve performance.

3. Balanced Approach:

Combine performance-based pay with other forms of compensation and employee benefits.

4. Fair and Transparent Processes:

Ensure the evaluation process is fair, transparent, and consistent across the organization.

Performance-based pay can be a powerful tool for motivating employees and driving business success, but it needs to be implemented thoughtfully and fairly to be effective. Organizations must balance motivation and reward with a healthy work environment and a focus on long-term goals.

Performance appraisal systems and their impact on compensation:

Explanation of how performance appraisals contribute to determining compensation levels.

Performance appraisal systems are critical tools used by organizations to evaluate employee performance, usually on an annual or semi-annual basis. These systems directly impact compensation, as they often form the basis for decisions regarding salary increases, bonuses, promotions, and sometimes disciplinary actions or terminations. Let's delve into how performance appraisals contribute to determining compensation levels and their overall impact.

Types of Performance Appraisal Systems:

1. 360-Degree Feedback:

Involves feedback from a variety of sources, including supervisors, peers, subordinates, and sometimes clients.

2. Management by Objectives (MBO):

Focuses on setting specific measurable goals and evaluating performance based on the achievement of these goals.

3. Rating Scale Method:

Employees are rated against specific criteria on a scale.

(e.g.1 to 5)

4. Behaviourally Anchored Rating Scales (BARS):

Combines elements of rating scales and critical incidents by directly tying the employee's performance ratings to specific behavioural examples.

5. Self-Evaluation:

Employees assess their performance, often to be discussed in a review meeting with their manager.

Impact on Compensation:

1. Merit-Based Increases:

Performance appraisals are typically used to determine merit-based salary increases. High performers may receive larger raises, while average or below-average performers receive smaller raises or none at all.

2. Bonuses and Incentives:

Many companies use appraisal outcomes to decide eligibility for bonuses. Employees who meet or exceed their targets or performance metrics are often rewarded with one-time bonuses.

3. Promotions:

Appraisals can identify employees ready for advancement and increased responsibilities, often accompanied by a salary increase.

4. Pay-for-Performance Culture:

In some organizations, particularly in sales or target-driven environments, compensation might be heavily influenced by appraisal outcomes, fostering a pay-for-performance culture.

Determining Compensation Levels:

1. Setting Performance Benchmarks:

Appraisals set clear performance benchmarks and expectations. Compensation is then aligned with these benchmarks.

2. Quantitative and Qualitative Measures:

Compensation adjustments are based on both quantitative results (e.g., sales figures, project completion) and qualitative aspects (e.g. teamwork, leadership qualities).

3. Consistency and Fairness:

A well-structured appraisal system aims to ensure consistency and fairness in compensation decisions, basing them on objective data and comprehensive evaluations.

Considerations and Challenges:

1. Subjectivity and Bias:

Appraisal systems can be subject to personal biases. Organizations need to ensure that appraisals are as objective and fair as possible.

2. Performance Measurement Complexity:

In roles where performance is not easily quantifiable, determining compensation adjustments can be challenging.

3. Communication:

Effective communication about how performance impacts compensation is crucial. Employees need to understand how their performance appraisal scores translate into salary increases or bonuses.

4. Continuous Feedback:

Relying solely on annual appraisals for compensation decisions can be limiting. More organizations are moving towards continuous feedback models to supplement traditional appraisals.

5. Legal Compliance:

Compensation decisions based on appraisals must comply with employment laws to avoid discrimination.

Performance appraisal systems play a pivotal role in determining compensation levels within organizations. They provide a structured way to assess performance and make informed compensation decisions. However, the effectiveness of these systems in driving fair and motivating compensation depends on their design, implementation, and the ongoing management of the appraisal process. Ensuring fairness, transparency, and alignment with organizational goals is key to leveraging performance appraisals as an effective tool for compensation management.

Considerations for Organizations:

1. Business Model:

Consider the nature of the business and whether it is sales-driven, innovation-focused, or requires a collaborative environment.

2. Organizational Culture:

Align the pay structure with the organization's values and culture. For example, a flat structure may suit a culture that values equality and collaboration.

3. Industry Norms:

Be aware of industry standards and practices to ensure competitiveness.

4. Talent Retention and Attraction:

Consider the impact of the chosen pay structure on talent retention and attraction. Some structures may be more appealing to certain demographics or job roles.

Conclusion

In conclusion, organizations decide on pay structures based on a combination of factors that align with their goals, values, and industry practices. It's important for organizations to regularly review and adapt their pay structures to remain competitive and responsive to evolving business needs.

"Recognizing and rewarding effort leads to a motivated and engaged workforce."

Chapter 4

Payroll Processing

Welcome to the intricate world of payroll processing, where precision and accuracy are paramount. In this chapter, we embark on a journey through the essential functions and complexities of payroll management. From calculating wages and deductions to ensuring compliance with tax laws and regulations, payroll processing plays a vital role in ensuring employees receive timely and accurate compensation. We will explore the various steps involved in payroll processing, including data collection, payroll calculations, and disbursement of funds. Additionally, we will discuss the importance of payroll software and technology in streamlining processes and minimizing errors. Join us as we navigate the labyrinth of payroll processing and uncover best practices for ensuring smooth and efficient payroll operations.

Overview of Payroll Processes and Systems:

A step-by-step guide on how payroll processing works, from calculating deductions to distributing paychecks.

Payroll processing is a critical function that involves calculating and distributing employees' compensation, including salaries, taxes, and deductions.

Here's a step-by-step guide on how payroll processing typically works:

Step 1: Gather Employee Information

Employee Records:
Ensure you have accurate and up-to-date employee information, including personal details, tax forms (e.g., W-4 in the U.S.), and bank account information for direct deposit.

Step 2: Track Employee Work Hours and Attendance

Time and Attendance:

Record employee work hours, including regular hours, overtime, and any absences. This information may come from time cards, time-tracking software, or attendance records.

Step 3: Calculate Gross Pay:

Hourly Wages:
For hourly employees, multiply the hours worked by their hourly rate to calculate the gross pay.

Salary:
For salaried employees, divide the annual salary by the number of pay periods in a year.

Step 4: Deduct Pre-tax Contributions

401(k) Contributions, Health Insurance Premiums, etc.:
Subtract any pre-tax contributions, such as retirement plan contributions and health insurance premiums, from the gross pay.

Step 5: Calculate Taxes

Federal, State, and Local Taxes:
Calculate federal, state, and local income taxes based on the employee's taxable income and tax withholding information provided on their W-4 or equivalent form.

Social Security and Medicare Taxes:
Deduct Social Security and Medicare taxes based on applicable rates and wage limits.

Step 6: Deduct Post-Tax Contributions

Post-tax Deductions:
Subtract post-tax deductions, such as union dues or after-tax contributions to retirement plans.

Step 7: Calculate Net Pay

Net Pay:
Subtract all deductions from the adjusted gross pay to calculate the employee's net pay - the amount they will receive in their paychecks.

Step 8: Process Payments

Direct Deposit or Paychecks:
Distribute payments using the chosen method, whether it's direct deposit into employees' bank accounts or physical paychecks.

Step 9: Record and Report

Record Transactions:
Document all payroll transactions, including gross pay, deductions, and net pay, in the payroll system.

Generate Payroll Reports:
Create reports detailing employee earnings, taxes withheld, and other relevant payroll information for record-keeping and compliance purposes.

Step 10: Remit Taxes and Contributions

Tax Payments:
Remit the deducted federal, state, and local taxes, along with any employer contributions, to the respective tax authorities.

Step 11: Stay Compliant

Compliance Checks:
Regularly review and update payroll processes to ensure compliance with tax laws, labour regulations, and any changes in employee status or benefits.

Step 12: Year-End Processing

Generate W-2s and Other Forms:

At the end of the year, generate W-2 forms for employees, summarizing their annual earnings and tax withholdings.

Annual Reporting:
Submit required annual reports to tax authorities, such as W-2s to the Social Security Administration and employees.

Considerations for Employers:

1. Invest in Payroll Software:

Utilize payroll software to automate calculations, reduce errors, and streamline the payroll process.

2. Stay Informed:

Stay informed about changes in tax laws and labour regulations to ensure compliance.

3. Offer Employee Self-Service:

Implement an employee self-service portal where employees can access their pay stubs, and tax forms, and update personal information.

4. Document Policies:

Document and communicate payroll policies, including deadlines, procedures, and the timing of payments.

By following these steps, organizations can ensure accurate and timely payroll processing, fostering employee satisfaction and regulatory compliance.

Legal and Regulatory Considerations in Payroll:

Under this sub-heading, we are going to highlight the importance of compliance with tax regulations, labour laws, and other legal considerations in payroll as it is paramount for any organization. This compliance not only ensures legal and ethical adherence to various statutory requirements but also protects the company from potential legal disputes, financial penalties, and reputational damage.

Here are the key reasons why compliance in payroll is so important:

1. Avoidance of Legal and Financial Penalties:

Non-compliance Consequences:
Failing to adhere to tax laws and labour regulations can lead to severe penalties, including fines and legal sanctions. These penalties can be significant and may even threaten the financial stability of a business.

Example:
In the U.S., failure to deposit payroll taxes can result in hefty fines and interest charges from the Internal Revenue Service

2. Adherence to Labor Laws:

Fair Labor Standards:
Compliance with labour laws, such as minimum wage requirements, overtime pay, and child labour laws, ensures fair treatment of employees. This is crucial for maintaining ethical business practices.

Example:
The Fair Labor Standards Act (FLSA) in the U.S. sets minimum wage, overtime pay eligibility, recordkeeping, and child labour standards.

3. Avoiding Litigation:

Employee Lawsuits:
Non-compliance can lead to employee lawsuits, which can be costly and time-consuming. These lawsuits may pertain to unpaid overtime, wage disputes, or wrongful deductions.

Example:

Class action lawsuits against companies for failing to pay overtime or misclassifying employees as exempt from overtime.

4. Maintaining Employee Trust and Morale:

Workplace Harmony:
Compliance ensures employees are paid fairly and on time, contributing to higher morale and trust in the employer. This is essential for a productive and harmonious workplace.

Example:
Regular and accurate payment of wages and benefits helps maintain positive employee relations and reduces turnover.

5. Upholding Company Reputation:

Public Image:
Adherence to legal standards helps in maintaining a positive public image. Non-compliance can result in negative publicity, affecting customer trust and investor confidence.

Example:
A company found violating labour laws may face public backlash and loss of business.

6. Ensuring Record-Keeping and Reporting Accuracy:

Documentation Compliance:
Accurate record-keeping and reporting are required for compliance. This involves maintaining detailed payroll records, tax filings, and compliance with reporting standards.

Example:
In many jurisdictions, employers are required to keep detailed payroll records for several years.

7. International Compliance:

Global Operations:
For businesses operating internationally, compliance becomes more complex due to varying tax laws and labour regulations in different countries.

Example:
A multinational corporation must comply with the tax and employment laws of each country it operates in.

8. Adapting to Legislative Changes:

Staying Informed:
Tax laws and labour regulations are subject to change. Organizations must stay informed and adapt their payroll systems to remain compliant.

Example:
Changes in tax rates or filing procedures require payroll systems to be updated accordingly.

Conclusion

Compliance in payroll is not just a legal obligation but a fundamental component of responsible business management. It requires constant vigilance, knowledge of current laws, and a proactive approach to ensure that all payroll processes are in line with legal requirements. This diligence helps safeguard the organization against legal risks, fosters a positive work environment, and upholds the organization's integrity and reputation.

"A well-compensated workforce is the engine that drives innovation and growth."

Chapter 5

Compensation Benchmarking

Welcome to the realm of compensation benchmarking, where organizations strive to ensure their compensation practices remain competitive and equitable. In this chapter, we delve into the process of comparing an organization's compensation packages with those of similar companies in the industry. Through benchmarking, organizations gain valuable insights into prevailing market trends, salary structures, and benefit offerings. By aligning their compensation strategies with industry standards, organizations can attract and retain top talent while maintaining cost efficiency. Join us as we explore the intricacies of compensation benchmarking and discover how it can drive strategic decision-making and enhance employee satisfaction.

Determining competitive salaries:

In this chapter, we try to understand how organizations determine competitive salaries. – Let us discuss the process of benchmarking against industry standards to ensure that an organization's compensation is competitive.

Determining competitive salaries is a crucial aspect of talent management for organizations. To ensure that compensation packages are competitive, organizations often engage in benchmarking against industry standards. This involves comparing their salary and benefits offerings with those of other companies in the same industry or region. Here's a detailed overview of the process:

How Organizations Determine Competitive Salaries:

1. Market Research:

Organizations conduct comprehensive market research to understand industry salary trends and benchmarks. This involves gathering data on compensation practices for similar roles within comparable organizations in the same geographical region or industry.

2. Compensation Surveys:

Participating in or purchasing compensation surveys is a common practice. These surveys provide data on salary ranges, benefits, and other compensation-related information. Sources include industry associations, consulting firms, and government reports.

3. Job Analysis and Evaluation:

Conducting a job analysis to understand the responsibilities, requirements, and qualifications for each position. Job evaluation methods, such as point-factor systems, may be used to assign a relative value to each job within the organization.

4. Internal Equity:

Ensuring internal equity by comparing the value of different jobs within the organization. Establishing a fair and consistent pay structure based on the relative worth of each position helps maintain a balanced and equitable compensation system.

5. Legal Compliance:

Adhering to legal requirements related to compensation, such as minimum wage laws, equal pay regulations, and other labour laws. Compliance ensures that the organization's compensation practices align with legal standards.

6. Employee Value Proposition (EVP):

Considering the organization's Employee Value Proposition, which includes not just monetary compensation but also non-monetary benefits and opportunities for professional development and growth.

7. Employee Surveys and Feedback:

Collecting feedback from employees through surveys or other means to understand their perceptions of the organization's compensation relative to the market. This helps in addressing employee concerns and improving retention.

Benchmarking Against Industry Standards:

Benchmarking against industry standards involves comparing the organization's compensation practices with those of similar organizations to ensure competitiveness. Here's the process:

1. Identify Comparable Organizations:

Select organizations that are similar in terms of industry, size, location, and other relevant factors. This ensures a meaningful comparison.

2. Gather Compensation Data:

Collect data on the compensation practices of the selected comparable organizations. This data includes salary ranges, benefits, bonuses, and any other relevant compensation components.

3. Analyse and Compare:

Analyse the gathered data to understand how the organization's compensation packages compare with industry standards. Identify areas where the organization may be lagging or excelling.

4. Adjust for Differences:

Consider factors that might differ between the organization and its benchmarks, such as company size, geographic location, or industry-specific challenges. Adjust the data accordingly for a more accurate comparison.

5. Set Competitive Salary Structures:

Based on the analysis, adjust the organization's salary structures to align with industry standards. This may involve making changes to base salaries, bonuses, or other incentive programs.

6. Regular Review and Updating:

Compensation benchmarking is an ongoing process. Regularly review and update the organization's compensation structures to remain competitive in the dynamic job market.

Importance of Competitive Salaries:

1. Attracting Top Talent:

Competitive salaries are crucial for attracting and retaining top talent in the industry. Job seekers often consider compensation as a key factor when evaluating job offers.

2. Retention of Skilled Employees:

Offering competitive salaries helps in retaining skilled and experienced employees, reducing turnover and associated costs.

3. Motivation and Job Satisfaction:

Competitive compensation contributes to employee motivation and job satisfaction, leading to increased productivity and engagement.

4. Market Positioning:

Organizations with competitive compensation packages enhance their market positioning and employer brand, making them more attractive to potential candidates.

5. Legal Compliance:

Ensuring that compensation is competitive also helps in compliance with labour laws and regulations, reducing the risk of legal issues related to compensation practices.

Determining competitive salaries involves a strategic approach that includes market research, benchmarking against industry standards, and regular reviews to stay aligned with market trends. This ensures that organizations remain competitive in the talent market and can attract, retain, and motivate a high-performing workforce.

Importance of benchmarking against industry standards:

Why staying informed about market trends is crucial in maintaining an effective salary system.

Benchmarking against industry standards is a critical practice for organizations aiming to establish and maintain effective salary systems. Staying informed about market trends through benchmarking provides valuable insights that are crucial for attracting, retaining, and motivating a talented workforce. Here's a detailed exploration of the importance of benchmarking against industry standards:

1. Attracting Top Talent:

Importance:
Job seekers often compare compensation packages when evaluating job offers. Offering salaries that are competitive with industry standards is essential for attracting top talent.

Impact:
Organizations that benchmark effectively and offer competitive salaries have a better chance of attracting skilled professionals and outperforming competitors in the talent market.

2. Retaining Skilled Employees:

Importance:

Competitive compensation is a key factor in retaining skilled and experienced employees. When employees feel they are fairly compensated, they are more likely to stay with the organization.

Impact:
Reducing turnover by retaining valuable employees not only saves recruitment and training costs but also contributes to organizational stability and knowledge retention.

3. Motivation and Job Satisfaction:

Importance:
Employees who believe they are compensated fairly are more likely to be motivated and satisfied in their roles. Compensation is a significant factor in overall job satisfaction.

Impact:
A motivated and satisfied workforce tends to be more engaged, productive, and committed to achieving organizational goals.

4. Market Positioning and Employer Brand:

Importance:
Competitive salaries contribute to an organization's market positioning and employer brand. A positive employer brand enhances the organization's reputation in the job market.

Impact:
Organizations with a strong employer brand are more likely to be the preferred choice for potential candidates, leading to a larger pool of high-quality applicants.

5. Legal Compliance:

Importance:

Staying informed about industry standards helps organizations ensure legal compliance with labour laws and regulations. This reduces the risk of legal issues related to compensation practices.

Impact:
Compliance with legal standards is crucial for avoiding penalties, lawsuits, and reputational damage.

6. Cost-Effective Recruitment and Retention:

Importance:
Offering competitive salaries reduces the need for frequent recruitment and onboarding, leading to cost savings. It's more cost-effective to retain skilled employees than to constantly replace them.

Impact:
By aligning salaries with industry standards, organizations can create a stable workforce, reducing the need for constant recruitment efforts.

7. Employee Morale and Trust:

Importance:
Transparency in compensation practices and alignment with industry standards build trust and morale among employees. They are more likely to trust the organization when they perceive fairness in pay.

Impact:
Higher morale contributes to a positive work environment, fosters collaboration, and strengthens the overall culture of the organization.

8. Strategic Decision-Making:

Importance:
Benchmarking against industry standards provides organizations with data-driven insights for strategic decision-making. It helps in determining competitive salary structures that align with business goals.

Impact:
Informed decision-making ensures that the organization remains adaptable and responsive to changes in the job market and economic conditions.

9. Talent Development and Succession Planning:

Importance:
Benchmarking allows organizations to assess how their compensation practices impact talent development and succession planning. It helps in identifying areas for improvement and growth.

Impact:
Effective talent development and succession planning contribute to the organization's long-term sustainability and leadership pipeline.

Conclusion

In conclusion, benchmarking against industry standards is crucial for maintaining an effective salary system. It enables organizations to align their compensation practices with market trends, attract and retain top talent, and make informed strategic decisions. By staying informed about industry standards, organizations position themselves as employers of choice, fostering a positive work environment and contributing to long-term success.

"Investing in your team's financial well-being pays dividends in loyalty and productivity."

Chapter 6

Negotiation and Salary Discussions

Embark on a journey into the art of negotiation and the nuances of salary discussions. In this chapter, we navigate the delicate balance between employers and employees as they engage in dialogues about compensation. From understanding negotiation tactics to mastering the art of articulating your worth, we uncover the strategies that lead to successful outcomes. Whether you're a seasoned professional or entering the workforce for the first time, this chapter equips you with the tools and insights to navigate salary discussions with confidence and poise. Join us as we unravel the complexities of negotiation and empower you to advocate for your value in the workplace.

Tips for employees negotiating salaries:

Here are some strategies for employees negotiating their salaries, including research, confidence, and effective communication. Negotiating a salary can be a critical moment in an employee's career journey. Effective negotiation requires preparation, confidence, and clear communication.

Some strategies for employees to navigate these discussions successfully.

1. Conduct Thorough Research:

Understand Your Worth:
Research the average salary for your position in your industry and region. Use websites like Glassdoor, PayScale, and LinkedIn Salary to gather this information.

Know the Company:
Understand the financial health and pay standards of the company. Smaller companies might not match the salaries of larger corporations, but they might offer other benefits.

Consider Your Experience:

Factor in your unique skills, experience, and qualifications. If you have in-demand skills or extensive experience, you might command a higher salary.

2. Prepare Your Case:

Document Your Achievements:
Compile a list of your achievements, particularly those that have positively impacted the company's bottom line or performance.

Quantify Your Value:
Where possible, use numbers and statistics to demonstrate how your work has contributed to the organization.

Develop a Proposal:
Prepare a clear and concise proposal that outlines your requested salary and the reasons you believe it is justified.

3. Build Confidence:

Practice Your Pitch:
Rehearse your proposal, either in front of a mirror or with a friend or family member. Being well-prepared will boost your confidence.

Mind-set Matters:
Remind yourself of your professional worth and the value you bring to the company. Confidence is key in negotiations.

Be Ready for Questions:
Anticipate potential counterarguments or questions and prepare your responses.

4. Effective Communication:

Be Clear and Direct:
When discussing your salary, be direct about your expectations. Use clear and professional language.

Listen Actively:
Pay attention to what the other party is saying. Understanding their perspective can help you address their concerns and adjust your proposal if necessary.

Non-Verbal Cues:
Be mindful of your body language. Maintain eye contact, sit up straight, and use gestures that convey confidence.

5. Be Flexible and Open to Compromise:

Consider Other Benefits:
If the employer cannot meet your salary expectations, consider negotiating for other benefits like flexible working hours, additional vacation time, or professional development opportunities.

Have a Range:
Instead of a single figure, have a salary range in mind. This shows that you are flexible and open to discussion.

6. Choose the Right Timing:

Performance Reviews:
These are often a good time for salary negotiations, especially if you have had a positive review.

After a Major Achievement:
If you have recently completed a major project or exceeded targets, it could be a good time to discuss a salary increase.

7. Handle Rejection Professionally:

Stay Calm:
If the answer is no, don't let your emotions take over. Ask for feedback and the reasons behind the decision.

Plan for the Future:

If a raise isn't possible now, discuss what you can do to achieve it in the future. Set goals and a timeline for a future review.

8. Follow Up in Writing:

Summarize Agreements:
After the negotiation, send an email summarizing the agreed terms (or the action plan if the negotiation will continue at a later date).

Salary negotiations can be challenging, but with the right preparation and approach, employees can navigate these discussions effectively. By doing thorough research, preparing a solid case, communicating effectively, and maintaining a professional demeanour, employees can enhance their chances of a successful negotiation.

Strategies for Employers in Salary Discussions:

Guidance for employers on how to navigate salary discussions, considering budget constraints and fairness:

Navigating salary discussions is a crucial task for employers, requiring a balance between organizational budget constraints and the need to be fair and competitive in compensation.

Here are strategies for employers to effectively handle these discussions:

1. Conduct Market Research:

Understand Industry Standards:
Regularly research and understand the going rates for various positions within your industry and region. This ensures your offers are competitive and fair.

Benchmark Salaries:
Regularly compare your salary scales against industry benchmarks to ensure they remain competitive and relevant.

2. Transparent Communication:

Be Open About Budget Constraints:
If there are budget limitations, be transparent about them. Employees appreciate honesty and understanding the company's financial context can set realistic expectations.

Explain Compensation Structures:
Help employees understand how salaries are structured and determined within your organization. This includes base pay, bonuses, and any performance-related incentives.

3. Prepare and Train Management:

Equip Managers:
Ensure that managers who handle salary negotiations are well-trained and understand the company's compensation philosophy, policies, and constraints.

Consistent Messaging:
All managers must convey a consistent message about compensation to avoid misunderstandings and perceptions of unfairness.

4. Focus on Total Compensation:

Highlight the Full Package:
Sometimes, salary isn't everything.

Emphasize the total compensation package, including benefits like health insurance, retirement plans, paid time off, flexible working conditions, and opportunities for professional development.

Tailor Benefits:
Understand what might be valuable to different employees (e.g., childcare support might be more valuable to a young parent than a gym membership).

5. Establish Clear Performance Metrics:

Link Pay to Performance:

Have clear, measurable performance indicators that are linked to salary increments or bonuses. This makes salary discussions more objective and merit-based.

Regular Reviews:
Implement a system of regular performance reviews to discuss not just salary, but overall career progression.

6. Negotiation Flexibility:

Be Open to Negotiation:
Understand that salary discussions are a negotiation. Be prepared to listen to employee requests and be open to compromise where possible.

Alternative Compensation:
If unable to meet salary demands, consider non-monetary compensation or benefits that could be equally motivating.

7. Maintain Fairness and Equity:

Ensure Equity:
Regularly review your salary structures to ensure they are fair and equitable across all levels of the organization. Address any disparities that may arise.

Avoid Bias:
Ensure that salary decisions are free from bias and based solely on role, experience, performance, and market standards.

8. Plan for Future Discussions:

Set Future Goals:
If an immediate salary increase is not feasible, work with the employee to set clear goals and a timeline for when a raise can be revisited.

Career Development Focus:
Discuss career development paths and how they can lead to salary increases in the future.

9. Document Agreements:

Follow-Up in Writing:
After a salary discussion, document what was agreed upon and provided to the employee for their records.

Conclusion

For employers, salary discussions are not just about negotiating figures but are also an opportunity to reinforce the organization's values, ensure fairness, and demonstrate appreciation for employee contributions. Balancing budget constraints with competitive compensation requires transparent communication, a clear understanding of the market, and a focus on total employee well-being. By adopting these strategies, employers can navigate salary discussions effectively, leading to a more motivated and committed workforce.

"In a fair compensation structure, everyone wins – employees, employers, and the business itself."

70

Chapter 7

Legal and Ethical Considerations

Delve into the legal and ethical dimensions of compensation management in this enlightening chapter. As organizations navigate the intricate landscape of employment laws and regulations, it becomes imperative to uphold ethical standards while ensuring compliance with legal requirements. From understanding labor laws to addressing issues of pay equity and diversity, we explore the principles that underpin fair and ethical compensation practices. Join us as we navigate the complexities of employment law and ethics, empowering organizations to foster a workplace culture built on integrity, fairness, and respect for all employees.

Anti-discrimination laws related to compensation:

This chapter discusses laws related to equal pay and discrimination to ensure a fair and equitable salary system.

In India, as well as in other major developing countries, several anti-discrimination laws and regulations are in place to address issues related to compensation, equal pay, and workplace discrimination. The goal is to promote fair and equitable salary systems, eliminate gender-based wage gaps, and ensure that all employees are treated fairly.

Below are key aspects of anti-discrimination laws related to compensation in India and some insights into the broader landscape in major developing countries:

India:

1. Equal Remuneration Act, 1976:

The Equal Remuneration Act prohibits discrimination in wages based on gender. It ensures that men and women receive equal pay for the same work or work of a similar nature.

Employers are required to provide equal wages for the same or similar work and are prohibited from discriminating against employees based on gender in matters of recruitment, training, and promotions.

2. Sexual Harassment of Women at Workplace (Prevention, Prohibition, and Redressal) Act, 2013:

While primarily addressing sexual harassment, this act indirectly contributes to a fair work environment by ensuring that victims of harassment are not subjected to discrimination in terms of their compensation or career advancement.

3. Labor Laws:

Various labour laws in India, such as the Minimum Wages Act, the Payment of Bonus Act, and the Industrial Employment (Standing Orders) Act, contain provisions that contribute to ensuring fair compensation practices.

4. Corporate Governance Guidelines:

SEBI (Securities and Exchange Board of India) has introduced corporate governance guidelines that encourage companies to disclose information related to the remuneration of directors and key managerial personnel to promote transparency and fairness.

Other Major Developing Countries (General Insights):

1. Equal Pay Legislation:

Many developing countries have specific laws addressing equal pay for equal work or work of equal value, aiming to eliminate gender-based wage discrimination. These laws often prohibit employers from paying employees differently based on gender for the same or similar work.

2. Labour Codes and Legislation:

Labour codes and various employment-related legislation in developing countries typically include provisions related to fair wages, non-discrimination, and equal opportunities. These may cover aspects such as recruitment, promotion, and benefits.

3. Constitutional Protections:

Constitutional provisions in several countries ensure equal protection under the law, which can extend to protection against discrimination in the workplace, including in matters of compensation.

4. Global Initiatives:

Global initiatives and conventions, such as those by the International Labour Organization (ILO), set standards for fair labour practices and non-discrimination in compensation. Many developing countries align their legislation with these international standards.

Laws regarding social and financial equality within the company/organization in various countries including India with their objectives and key features

[Here is an overview with objectives and key features of laws, but please note that it's important to consult legal professionals for the most up-to-date and accurate information.]

India:

1. Equal Remuneration Act, 1976:

Objective:
Ensures equal pay for equal work between male and female employees.

Key Features:
Prohibits discrimination based on gender in remuneration and recruitment.

2. Maternity Benefit Act, 1961:

Objective:
Protects the employment of women during maternity and entitles them to maternity benefits.

Key Features:
Grants maternity leave, medical benefits, and other related provisions.

3. Companies Act, 2013:

Objective:
Encourages corporate social responsibility (CSR) activities by certain companies.

Key Features:
Requires eligible companies to spend a percentage of their profits on CSR initiatives, promoting social equality.

4. Scheduled Castes and Tribes (Prevention of Atrocities) Act, 1989:

Objective:
Prevents atrocities against individuals belonging to Scheduled Castes and Scheduled Tribes.

Key Features:
Penalizes discrimination and violence against marginalized communities.

5. Sexual Harassment of Women at Workplace (Prevention, Prohibition, and Redressal) Act, 2013:

Objective:
Addresses sexual harassment of women in the workplace.

Key Features:

Mandates the establishment of Internal Complaints Committees (ICC) and prescribes procedures for addressing complaints.

United States:

1. Equal Pay Act of 1963:

Objective:
Prohibits wage discrimination based on gender.

Key Features:
Mandates that men and women be given equal pay for equal work in the same establishment.

2. Civil Rights Act of 1964:

Objective:
Prohibits discrimination based on race, colour, religion, sex, or national origin.

Key Features:
Title VII specifically addresses workplace discrimination, promoting social and racial equality.

3. Americans with Disabilities Act (ADA):

Objective:
Prohibits discrimination against individuals with disabilities.

Key Features:
Requires employers to provide reasonable accommodations for employees with disabilities.

4. Family and Medical Leave Act (FMLA):

Objective:
Allows eligible employees to take unpaid leave for certain family or medical reasons.

Key Features:
Aims to balance the demands of the workplace with the needs of families.

United Kingdom:

1. Equality Act 2010:

Objective:
Ensures equal opportunities and combats discrimination in the workplace.

Key Features:
Protects individuals from discrimination based on characteristics such as age, disability, gender, race, and religion.

2. National Minimum Wage Act 1998:

Objective:
Sets the minimum wage for workers.

Key Features:
Ensures that workers receive fair and equitable compensation.

3. Gender Pay Gap Reporting Regulations:

Objective:
Requires large employers to publish information on the gender pay gap.

Key Features:
Promotes transparency and addresses gender-based pay disparities.

Each country has its own set of laws and regulations aimed at fostering social and financial equality within organizations. Employers need to be aware of and comply with these laws to create inclusive and equitable workplaces. It's crucial to stay updated on any changes in legislation and seek legal advice to ensure full compliance.

Challenges and Areas for Improvement:

1. Implementation and Enforcement:

One challenge in many developing countries is the effective implementation and enforcement of anti-discrimination laws. There may be gaps in enforcement mechanisms or insufficient resources for monitoring compliance.

2. Awareness and Sensitization:

Raising awareness about anti-discrimination laws, equal pay, and fair compensation practices is crucial. Many employees may not be fully aware of their rights, and employers may need more education on creating inclusive workplaces.

3. Intersectionality:

Addressing intersectional aspects of discrimination (such as race, ethnicity, and other factors) is essential to ensure a comprehensive approach to workplace fairness and equity.

4. Regular Review and Updating:

Legislation needs to be regularly reviewed and updated to keep pace with evolving societal norms and economic conditions. This includes considering new forms of work, such as gig work, and their implications for compensation.

Anti-discrimination laws related to compensation play a crucial role in fostering fair and equitable salary systems in India and other major developing countries. While progress has been made, ongoing efforts are needed to address challenges, enhance awareness, and strengthen enforcement mechanisms to ensure that all employees are treated fairly and have equal opportunities in the workplace.

Ensuring Fairness and equity in salary distribution:

The importance of fairness and equity in salary distribution to maintain a positive workplace culture. Maintaining fairness and equity in salary distribution is paramount for fostering a positive workplace culture. A compensation system that prioritizes fairness and equity contributes to employee satisfaction, engagement, and overall well-being.

Here are key reasons highlighting the importance of fairness and equity in salary distribution:

1. Employee Morale and Satisfaction:

Positive Impact:
Fair and equitable salary distribution boosts employee morale, leading to higher job satisfaction.

When employees feel that their compensation is fair, they are more likely to be motivated and committed to their work.

2. Retention of Top Talent:

Attracting and Retaining Talent:
A fair salary structure is a powerful tool for attracting and retaining top talent.

Employees are more likely to stay with an organization that values and compensates their contributions appropriately.

3. Reduced Turnover:

Cost Savings:
Fair and equitable compensation helps in reducing turnover. High employee turnover is costly for organizations in terms of recruitment, onboarding, and lost productivity.

A stable workforce contributes to cost savings and organizational stability.

4. Enhanced Employee Engagement:

Alignment with Organizational Goals:
Fair compensation aligns employee efforts with organizational goals. When employees perceive that their contributions are recognized and rewarded, they are more engaged and committed to achieving shared objectives.

5. Improved Productivity:

Motivation and Performance:
Fair compensation is a motivator for employees to perform at their best. When employees feel they are being compensated fairly, they are more likely to go the extra mile, leading to improved overall productivity.

6. Positive Organizational Culture:

Trust and Collaboration:
Fairness in salary distribution fosters a culture of trust and collaboration.

When employees trust that they are being treated fairly, it creates a positive and supportive work environment.

7. Diversity and Inclusion:

Addressing Pay Disparities:
A commitment to fairness and equity helps address pay disparities, contributing to a more inclusive workplace.

This is essential for attracting and retaining a diverse workforce.

8. Compliance with Legal and Ethical Standards:

Legal and Ethical Obligations:
Fair salary distribution ensures compliance with legal and ethical standards.

It helps organizations avoid legal issues related to discrimination and promotes ethical business practices.

9. Employee Well-Being:

Financial Stability:
Fair compensation is crucial for the financial stability and well-being of employees.

It enables them to meet their basic needs, reduce financial stress, and focus on personal and professional growth.

10. Organizational Reputation:

Employer Branding:
Organizations that prioritize fairness in salary distribution build a positive employer brand.

A strong reputation as an employer of choice attracts top talent and enhances the organization's standing in the market.

11. Adaptability and Innovation:

Encouraging Innovation:
A fair compensation system encourages innovation and creativity. Employees are more likely to contribute new ideas and take risks when they feel their efforts are valued.

12. Employee Loyalty:

Long-Term Commitment:
Fair and equitable compensation builds a sense of loyalty among employees.

Loyalty is a valuable asset for organizations, contributing to long-term stability and success.

Conclusion

Fairness and equity in salary distribution are foundational elements of a positive workplace culture. Organizations that prioritize these principles not only attract and retain top talent but also create an environment where employees feel valued, motivated, and engaged. This, in turn, contributes to higher productivity, organizational success, and a positive reputation in the marketplace.

"Rewarding excellence breeds a culture of success."

Chapter 8

Emerging Trends in Compensation

Embark on a journey into the future of compensation management in this forward-thinking chapter. As the business landscape evolves, so too do the practices and strategies surrounding employee compensation. Explore cutting-edge trends such as flexible compensation packages, performance-based incentives, and the rise of remote work allowances. From embracing technology-driven solutions to addressing the changing needs and expectations of the workforce, we delve into the innovative approaches that are shaping the future of compensation. Join us as we navigate the forefront of compensation management, empowering organizations to stay ahead of the curve and attract top talent in an ever-evolving marketplace.

Remote work and its impact on salary structures:

Let us discuss on how the rise of remote work is influencing salary structures. The rise of remote work has brought about significant changes in how companies structure their salary offerings. As more organizations adopt or expand remote work policies, they are re-evaluating their compensation strategies to address the unique challenges and opportunities presented by remote work.

Here's an exploration of how remote work is influencing salary structures:

1. Location-Agnostic Compensation:

Traditional vs. Remote:
In traditional office setups, compensation often considers the cost of living in the location where the employee works. However, with remote work, some companies are moving toward location-agnostic or "geo-blind" compensation models.

[What is Geo-Blind Compensation Model:

The term "geo-blind compensation model" refers to a pay structure that disregards an employee's geographical location when determining their salary or compensation package. Instead, compensation is based solely on factors such as job role, skills, experience, and performance, without taking into account the cost of living or prevailing wage rates in the employee's location. In a geo-blind compensation model, employees performing the same role with similar qualifications and responsibilities are paid equally regardless of where they are located. This approach aims to promote fairness and equity within an organization by ensuring that employees are compensated based on their contributions rather than their geographic location.

For example, suppose a software company adopts a geo-blind compensation model for its remote workforce. Regardless of whether an employee is based in a high-cost urban area like San Francisco or a lower-cost rural area, their salary is determined by factors such as their job title, skills, and experience level. This means that a software engineer working remotely from a small town would receive the same salary as a colleague with similar qualifications working in a major city, provided their job roles are identical.

By implementing a geo-blind compensation model, organizations can attract and retain talent based on merit rather than location, potentially reducing disparities in pay and promoting a more inclusive work environment. However, it's essential for companies to ensure that their compensation structures align with legal requirements and industry standards, particularly regarding minimum wage laws and fair pay practices.]

Equal Pay for Equal Work:
Location-agnostic compensation emphasizes paying employees based on their roles and responsibilities rather than their physical location, promoting the principle of equal pay for equal work.

2. Cost-of-Living Adjustments:

Re-evaluation of Adjustments:
Some companies are reconsidering or reducing cost-of-living adjustments for remote employees. This shift reflects the belief that remote employees should

be compensated based on the organization's overall pay scale rather than the cost of living in their specific region.

Equity Concerns:
However, this approach has raised concerns about potential equity issues, as employees in high-cost-of-living areas may feel they are unfairly affected.

3. Competitive Talent Market:

Global Talent Pool:
Remote work allows organizations to tap into a global talent pool. To attract top talent, companies may offer competitive salaries that align with industry standards rather than local averages.

Talent Mobility:
Remote work enables employees to work for companies based in different regions or countries. To remain competitive, organizations may adjust salary structures to accommodate this increased talent mobility.

4. Retention and Employee Satisfaction:

Retaining Remote Talent:
To retain remote talent, companies may offer competitive salaries and benefits. This is particularly important as skilled professionals, empowered by remote work, have more choices and may seek opportunities that offer better compensation.

Balancing Flexibility and Compensation:
Organizations are finding a balance between offering remote flexibility and maintaining competitive compensation to keep employees satisfied.

5. Remote Work Allowances:

Providing Remote Work Stipends:
Some companies offer remote work allowances or stipends to cover expenses related to creating a home office, such as internet costs, office furniture, and utilities. These allowances can be part of the overall compensation package.

6. Performance-Based Compensation:

Emphasis on Results:
Remote work often places a greater emphasis on results rather than time spent in the office. Performance-based compensation models, such as bonuses tied to measurable outcomes, are becoming more prevalent in remote work environments.

7. Market Research and Benchmarking:

Dynamic Market Conditions:
Remote work has led to dynamic shifts in the labour market. Companies are continuously conducting market research and benchmarking to understand how their compensation structures compare to industry standards and competitors.

8. Employee Benefits:

Flexible Benefits:
Remote work has prompted a re-evaluation of traditional employee benefits. Companies may offer flexible benefits packages, allowing employees to choose benefits that align with their individual needs, including health insurance, wellness programs, and professional development opportunities.

9. Tax Implications:

Cross-Border Considerations:
Remote work across borders introduces tax implications for both employees and employers. Companies are navigating these complexities and adjusting compensation structures to account for tax-related considerations.

10. Communication and Transparency:

Clear Communication:
Transparent communication about the factors influencing remote compensation is crucial. Companies are communicating their policies,

rationale, and any changes to ensure clarity and avoid misunderstandings among employees.

11. Legal and Compliance Considerations:

Adherence to Laws:
Remote work introduces legal complexities related to employment laws, taxation, and compliance. Companies are ensuring that their remote compensation practices align with local and international regulations. The impact of remote work on salary structures is a dynamic and evolving landscape. Organizations are adapting to the changing nature of work by rethinking how they compensate employees in remote settings. The key is finding the right balance between offering competitive salaries, ensuring fairness, and aligning compensation practices with the expectations and preferences of a remote workforce. As the remote work trend continues to shape the future of work, organizations will likely refine their approaches to compensation to meet the evolving needs of both employees and the business.

Trends in Flexible compensation and benefits:

Let us discuss on trends in flexible compensation, such as customizable benefits packages.

Flexible compensation and benefits have gained significant traction in the evolving landscape of work. This shift reflects the changing preferences and needs of a diverse workforce, where a one-size-fits-all approach to compensation is no longer effective.

Here's an in-depth look at the trends in flexible compensation and benefits:

1. Customizable Benefits Packages:

Employee Choice:
More companies are offering employees the opportunity to customize their benefits package. This approach allows employees to select from a variety of options, tailoring their benefits to meet their individual needs and lifestyles.

Options Offered:
These packages often include traditional benefits like health insurance and retirement plans, along with choices like wellness programs, mental health support, remote working allowances, childcare support, and educational assistance.

2. Wellness and Mental Health Programs:

Increased Focus:
There's an increasing emphasis on wellness and mental health programs. Recognizing the importance of employee well-being, companies are including gym memberships, yoga classes, mental health days, and access to counselling services as part of their benefits.

Remote Work Considerations:
As remote work becomes more prevalent, there's a trend towards offering benefits that support a healthy work-from-home environment, such as ergonomic furniture or allowances for setting up a home office.

3. Flexible Working Arrangements:

Hybrid Models:
Many organizations are embracing hybrid work models, allowing employees to split their time between home and office. This flexibility is increasingly seen as a key component of compensation packages.

Completely Remote Options:
Some companies are offering fully remote positions, appealing to talent who prefer or require this level of flexibility.

4. Financial Wellness Programs:

Educational Resources:
Employers are integrating financial wellness into their benefits, offering resources and tools for financial planning, debt management, and retirement savings.

Investment Options:
This can also include offering employees access to financial advisors or investment options that help in building long-term financial stability.

5. Performance-Based Incentives:

Results-Oriented Compensation:
There's a growing trend towards linking compensation more directly with performance, including the use of bonuses, profit sharing, and stock options.

Personalized Goals:
Performance metrics are increasingly being personalized to reflect individual roles and contributions, rather than relying on broad company-wide targets.

6. Education and Professional Development:

Career Advancement:
Recognizing the importance of ongoing learning, many employers are offering benefits related to education and professional development. This includes tuition reimbursement, access to online courses, and attendance at conferences and workshops.

Skills Development:
This trend reflects the need for continuous skill development in an ever-changing job market and can also help with employee retention.

7. Childcare and Family Benefits:

Support for Parents:
With the increasing number of dual-income households, employers are offering benefits that support working parents, such as on-site childcare, subsidies for childcare services, and flexible scheduling.

Parental Leave:
Enhanced maternity and paternity leave policies are also becoming more common.

8. Voluntary Benefits:

Additional Options:
Beyond the standard benefits package, companies are offering a range of voluntary benefits like pet insurance, legal assistance, and lifestyle spending accounts.

Employee-Paid Options:
These benefits are often employee-paid but come at a lower rate due to group discounts.

9. Technology Integration:

Benefits Platforms:
The use of technology platforms to manage and select benefits is on the rise. These platforms make it easier for employees to understand and choose their benefits, and for employers to administer them.

Personalized Experience:
AI and data analytics are being used to provide personalized benefit recommendations based on employee data and preferences.

Conclusion

The trend in flexible compensation and benefits reflects a broader shift towards more personalized and holistic approaches to employee compensation. As the workforce becomes increasingly diverse and the lines between work and personal life continue to blur, employers are recognizing the need to offer a range of benefits that cater to varied lifestyles and needs. This flexibility not only enhances employee satisfaction and well-being but also serves as a key differentiator in attracting and retaining talent in a competitive job market.

"Employee satisfaction is the true measure of a company's wealth."

Chapter 9

Case Studies and Examples

Unlock the power of real-world scenarios in this illuminating chapter, where theory meets practice. Dive deep into a collection of compelling case studies and examples that bring the principles of compensation management to life. From multinational corporations to small start-ups, explore how organizations across industries navigate the complexities of salary structures, employee benefits, and performance incentives. Witness first-hand the impact of strategic compensation decisions on employee satisfaction, retention, and organizational success. Through detailed analyses and insightful anecdotes, discover the key lessons and best practices gleaned from the experiences of leading companies. Whether you're seeking inspiration or practical insights, this chapter offers a treasure trove of knowledge to inform your compensation strategies and drive business excellence.

Successful salary systems:

Let us see some real-world examples of successful salary systems and real-world examples of organizations with effective compensation strategies.

Several organizations have implemented successful and innovative salary systems that align with their business goals, attract top talent, and retain high-performing employees.

Below are real-world examples of organizations with effective compensation strategies:

1. Netflix:

Performance-Based Culture

Strategy:
Netflix is known for its unique approach to compensation, emphasizing a performance-based culture. The company moved away from traditional annual

performance reviews and instead focused on real-time feedback and individual contributions.

Key Features:
High-performing employees are rewarded with higher compensation, and the company encourages a sense of ownership and responsibility. Netflix believes in paying top-of-market salaries to attract and retain the best talent.

2. Salesforce:

Equal Pay Certification

Strategy:
Salesforce has been a pioneer in addressing pay equity.

The company regularly conducts audits to ensure that employees are paid fairly regardless of gender. Salesforce is committed to achieving and maintaining equal pay for equal work.

Key Features:
The Company has received Equal Pay Certification from third-party organizations, demonstrating its dedication to eliminating gender-based pay disparities.

3. Google:

Total Compensation Package

Strategy:
Google is known for offering a comprehensive total compensation package that goes beyond traditional salary. The company provides a range of benefits, including health insurance, retirement plans, on-site amenities, and professional development opportunities.

Key Features:

Google's compensation strategy focuses on creating a holistic and attractive work environment, promoting employee well-being, and fostering a culture of innovation.

4. Costco:

Competitive Wages and Benefits

Strategy:
Costco is recognized for offering competitive wages and a generous benefits package to its employees. The company believes in investing in its workforce, paying higher-than-average wages, and providing comprehensive benefits.

Key Features:
Costco's strategy has resulted in high employee satisfaction, low turnover rates, and a positive reputation as an employer of choice in the retail industry.

5. Microsoft:

Performance Bonuses and Stock Options

Strategy:
Microsoft incorporates performance bonuses and stock options into its compensation structure. The company links employee compensation to individual and team performance, providing opportunities for employees to share in the company's success through stock ownership.

Key Features:
This strategy aligns the interests of employees with the company's long-term growth and performance, motivating employees to contribute to Microsoft's success.

6. HubSpot:

Transparent Compensation Philosophy

Strategy:

HubSpot has adopted a transparent compensation philosophy, openly sharing its pay scales and the factors that influence salary decisions. The company emphasizes fairness and equity in compensation and actively communicates its commitment to employees.

Key Features:
HubSpot's transparency fosters trust among employees, reduces ambiguity, and ensures that individuals understand how their contributions are valued in terms of compensation.

7. Zappos:

Holacracy and Unique Compensation Practices

Strategy:
Zappos has experimented with a unique organizational structure called Holacracy, which eliminates traditional hierarchies. The company also offers a compensation approach that includes profit sharing and a unique bonus structure.

Key Features:
Zappos' innovative practices focus on creating a dynamic and collaborative workplace where employees are motivated by a sense of autonomy and shared success.

8. Bridgewater Associates:

Performance-Based and Radical Transparency

Strategy:
Bridgewater Associates, an investment firm, has a performance-based compensation model and practices radical transparency. The company encourages open and direct feedback, and employees are compensated based on their contributions and performance.

Key Features:

Bridgewater Associates' approach aims to create a meritocratic environment, where decisions around compensation are based on objective measures of individual and team performance.

These real-world examples showcase the diversity of compensation strategies adopted by successful organizations. Whether it's a focus on performance-based cultures, equal pay initiatives, comprehensive total compensation packages, or unique organizational structures, effective compensation strategies align with the values and goals of the organization while prioritizing fairness, transparency, and employee well-being. Successful salary systems are those that not only attract top talent but also contribute to a positive workplace culture and long-term organizational success.

Now few examples from India

In India, several companies have implemented innovative and effective salary systems that cater to the unique needs of their workforce and business environment. Here are some notable examples:

1. Infosys:

Performance-Based Compensation and Stock Options

Strategy:
Infosys, a global leader in consulting, technology, and outsourcing, has a robust performance-based compensation structure. The company regularly assesses employee performance and aligns compensation with individual achievements.

Key Features:
Apart from salaries, Infosys offers performance bonuses, stock options, and long-term incentive plans, thereby creating a strong linkage between pay and performance.

2. Tata Consultancy Services (TCS):

Comprehensive Rewards System

Strategy:
TCS, one of India's largest IT services companies, has a comprehensive rewards system that goes beyond the basic salary. The system includes various benefits, performance incentives, and recognition programs.

Key Features:
The company focuses on recognizing both individual and team contributions, with bonuses and promotions based on performance metrics.

3. Hindustan Unilever (HUL):

Competitive Compensation and Career Growth Opportunities

Strategy:
HUL, known for its fast-moving consumer goods, offers competitive compensation packages. The company is known for providing excellent career growth opportunities, which are an integral part of its compensation strategy.

Key Features:
HUL provides various benefits, including health insurance, retirement plans, and flexible working options. It also emphasizes internal promotions and talent development, adding value to its compensation package.

[Unilever is a multinational consumer goods company. Unilever has its roots in the Lever Brothers company, which was founded in 1885 by William Hesketh Lever and his brother James Darcy Lever in the United Kingdom. Lever Brothers expanded rapidly, establishing operations in various countries around the world. In 1930, Lever Brothers merged with Margarine Unie, a Dutch margarine producer, to form Unilever. Unilever operates through various subsidiaries and divisions, organized geographically and by product category. The company has a complex corporate structure designed to manage its global operations effectively. Unilever has dual headquarters in Rotterdam, Netherlands, and London, United Kingdom. Unilever is led by a team of executives and board members responsible for overseeing the company's operations, strategy, and corporate governance. The leadership team includes individuals with diverse backgrounds and expertise in various areas of business.

Hindustan Unilever Limited (HUL) is indeed a part of Unilever. HUL is the Indian subsidiary of Unilever and operates as a separate entity under the umbrella of the larger Unilever company. While HUL manages its operations in India, it aligns with Unilever's global strategy and shares resources, technology, and expertise with the parent company. Hindustan Unilever Limited is headquartered in Mumbai, Maharashtra, India. As such, HUL benefits from Unilever's global scale and presence while catering to the specific needs of the Indian market.]

4. Wipro:

Employee Stock Ownership Plans (ESOPs)

Strategy:
Wipro, another major player in the IT sector, offers Employee Stock Ownership Plans (ESOPs) to its employees. This strategy is designed to align the interests of the employees with those of the company and its shareholders.

Key Features:
Wipro's compensation structure includes competitive salaries, bonuses, and various employee benefits, along with the ESOPs, to foster a sense of ownership among employees.

5. Reliance Industries:

Variable Pay and Bonuses

Strategy:
Reliance Industries, a conglomerate with diverse business interests, incorporates a significant variable pay component as part of its compensation structure. This includes performance-linked bonuses.

Key Features:
The Company's compensation system is designed to reward high performers and is closely tied to business objectives and individual contributions.

6. Godrej Group:

Holistic Employee Well-being

Strategy:
The Godrej Group, with interests in real estate, consumer products, and agribusiness, focuses on holistic employee well-being in its compensation strategy. The company offers a range of benefits aimed at physical, mental, and financial well-being.

Key Features:
Their comprehensive benefits package includes health care, retirement benefits, professional development opportunities, and work-life balance initiatives.

7. Flipkart:

Competitive Salaries and Start-up Culture

Strategy:
As one of India's leading e-commerce companies, Flipkart offers competitive salaries and embraces a start-up culture, attracting top talent in the technology and e-commerce sectors.

Key Features:
The Company provides a dynamic work environment with opportunities for rapid career progression, stock options, and a range of employee benefits.

These examples from India illustrate how companies are adopting diverse and innovative compensation strategies to attract, motivate, and retain talent. Whether it's through performance-based pay, comprehensive benefits, career development opportunities, or stock ownership plans, these strategies reflect the organizations' commitment to aligning employee interests with business goals while considering the holistic well-being of their workforce.

Case studies on organizations that have effectively managed compensations:

Let us dive into specific cases illustrating how companies manage compensation challenges. Effective compensation management is a critical aspect of organizational success. Below are detailed case studies of organizations that have successfully navigated compensation challenges, illustrating diverse strategies and approaches:

1. Salesforce:

Addressing Gender Pay Gap

Background:
Salesforce, a global leader in CRM software, faced the challenge of addressing the gender pay gap, a common issue in the tech industry.

Strategy:
The Company conducted comprehensive internal audits to assess and rectify pay disparities across genders.

Actions:

Analysed employee compensation data annually.

Adjusted salaries where discrepancies were found.

Implemented policies to maintain pay equity, including reviewing offers to new hires.

Outcome:
Salesforce spent millions of dollars to eliminate statistically significant pay differences. The company set a precedent in the tech industry for proactive measures towards pay equality.

Learning:
Regular audits and proactive adjustments are key to maintaining equitable compensation.

2. Walmart:

Wage Increases and Training Programs

Background:
Walmart, the world's largest retailer, faced criticism over low wages and poor working conditions.

Strategy:
To improve employee satisfaction and reduce turnover, Walmart increased its minimum wages and invested in employee training and development.

Actions:

Incrementally raised minimum wages.

Introduced training programs to enhance skills and career growth.

Linked wage growth to training milestones.

Outcome:
These changes led to improved employee morale, customer service, and a decrease in turnover rates.

Learning:
Investing in employee wages and development can yield long-term benefits in productivity and retention.

3. Netflix:

High Salary and Freedom and Responsibility

Background:
Netflix, facing intense competition for talent in Silicon Valley, needed a strategy to attract and retain top talent.

Strategy:
The Company adopted a unique compensation model, offering high salaries combined with a culture of freedom and responsibility.

Actions:

Offered top-of-the-market salaries.

Implemented a flexible, no-tracking vacation policy.

Encouraged independent decision-making and responsibility.

Outcome:
Netflix successfully attracted high-calibre talent, fostering a high-performance culture and supporting its rapid growth.

Learning:
Competitive pay combined with a positive culture can be a powerful tool in attracting and retaining talent.

4. Zappos:

Holacracy and Compensation

Background:
Zappos, an online shoe and clothing retailer, implemented a flat organizational structure called Holacracy, posing unique compensation challenges.

Strategy:
Zappos restructured its compensation system to fit a non-hierarchical model.

Actions:

Abolished traditional job titles and career ladders.

Implemented a skills-based pay system, where employees are paid for the skills they bring and acquire.

Outcome:

While the transition was challenging and met with mixed responses, it allowed Zappos to innovate in aligning compensation with its unique culture.

Learning:
Compensation systems must align with organizational structure and culture, even if they require unconventional approaches.

5. Google:

Competitive Salaries and Perks

Background:
Google operates in a highly competitive market for tech talent.

Strategy:
To attract and retain the best talent, Google offers competitive salaries and a wide range of benefits.

Actions:

Provides above-average industry salaries.

Offers comprehensive health care, retirement plans, and on-site amenities.

Focuses on work-life balance and employee well-being.

Outcome:
Google consistently ranks as one of the best places to work, with low turnover rates and high employee satisfaction.

Learning:
A holistic approach to compensation, including both financial and non-financial benefits, can create a highly attractive work environment.

These case studies demonstrate that effective compensation management is multifaceted, involving not just competitive pay, but also considerations of equity, company culture, employee development, and organizational structure. Regularly evaluating and adapting compensation strategies is crucial for addressing emerging challenges and aligning with evolving business goals and workforce expectations.

Let's have a look at some case studies from India

Organizations from India have effectively managed compensation challenges, showcasing unique strategies and solutions:

1. Infosys:

Performance-Based Compensation and Employee Retention

Background:
Infosys, a global leader in technology services and consulting, faced challenges in retaining top talent in the highly competitive IT industry.

Strategy:
Infosys implemented a performance-based compensation model to incentivize and retain high-performing employees.

Actions:

Linked a significant portion of employee compensation to performance outcomes.

Regularly revised salary structures to stay competitive in the market.

Offered stock options and variable pay based on company and individual performance.

Outcome:
This approach helped in reducing attrition rates and boosting employee morale and productivity.

Learning:
Aligning compensation with performance and market standards is crucial in retaining top talent in competitive sectors.

2. Tata Consultancy Services (TCS):

Skill-Based Compensation

Background:
TCS, a leading global IT services, consulting, and business solutions organization, needed to manage a diverse workforce with varying skill levels.

Strategy:
The Company adopted a skill-based compensation strategy to align pay with individual skill sets and market demand.

Actions:

Implemented a system that pays premiums for employees with niche and high-demand skills.

Regular training and upskilling programs were introduced to enhance employee skills.

Outcome:
This strategy not only helped in retaining critical talent but also encouraged employees to upskill, benefiting both the employees and the organization.

Learning:
A dynamic compensation system that rewards skill development can foster a culture of continuous learning and adaptation.

3. Hindustan Unilever Ltd (HUL):

Balancing Compensation and Sustainability

Background:
HUL, a leader in the FMCG sector, aimed to balance competitive compensation with sustainable business practices.

Strategy:
Integrated sustainability goals into its compensation policy, linking executive pay to sustainable business performance.

Actions:

Part of the senior executives' compensation was tied to achieving targets in environmental sustainability and social responsibility.

Adopted a transparent approach to report on sustainability goals and compensation linkage.

Outcome:
This approach reinforced HUL's commitment to sustainability, improving its brand reputation and employee engagement.

Learning:
Linking compensation to broader business goals like sustainability can enhance corporate reputation and employee motivation.

4. Reliance Industries:

Variable Pay and Diversified Portfolio

Background:
Reliance Industries, operating in various sectors like telecom, retail, and petrochemicals, faced the challenge of managing a diverse workforce.

Strategy:
Implemented a flexible compensation structure with a significant variable component linked to individual, team, and company performance.

Actions:

Introduced performance-linked bonuses and stock options.

Customized compensation packages for different sectors within the conglomerate.

Outcome:
This approach helped in aligning employee interests with company performance, leading to improved productivity and satisfaction.

Learning:
A diversified compensation strategy that caters to different sectors and performance metrics can effectively manage a varied workforce.

5. Wipro:

Competitive Compensation in IT Sector

Background:
Wipro, another giant in the IT sector, faced the challenge of attracting and retaining skilled professionals in a highly competitive market.

Strategy:
Focused on offering competitive compensation packages along with continuous learning opportunities.

Actions:

Competitive base salaries coupled with performance bonuses and stock options.

Invested in extensive training programs and skill development initiatives.

Outcome:

Wipro managed to maintain a low attrition rate and high employee satisfaction, marking it as an employer of choice in the IT industry.

Learning:
A combination of competitive pay, career growth opportunities, and a focus on continuous learning can effectively attract and retain talent.

Conclusion

These case studies from India reflect the importance of a strategic approach to compensation management. Whether it's through performance-linked pay, skill-based compensation, integrating sustainability goals, or offering competitive packages with growth opportunities, these companies demonstrate the effectiveness of aligning compensation strategies with organizational objectives and employee expectations. This alignment is key to fostering employee engagement, satisfaction, and overall business success.

"Compensate with respect; motivate with recognition."

Chapter 10

Future of Compensation

Step into the realm of tomorrow's compensation strategies, where innovation and foresight intersect to shape the future of work. In this chapter, we embark on a journey through the evolving landscape of employee compensation, exploring emerging trends and pioneering approaches poised to redefine the employer-employee relationship. From advancements in pay structures to the integration of technology-driven solutions, we uncover the dynamic forces driving change in the compensation landscape. Join us as we navigate the complexities of tomorrow's workforce, offering insights and strategies to help organizations stay ahead in an ever-evolving business environment.

In this chapter, we discuss on predictions and considerations for the future of salary systems. Insights and predictions on how compensation practices might evolve. Predicting the future of salary systems involves considering current trends, technological advancements, societal changes, and evolving workforce dynamics. While the future is inherently uncertain, here are some insights and predictions on how compensation practices might evolve:

1. Increased Emphasis on Total Well-being:

Prediction:

Organizations will expand their focus beyond traditional compensation components to incorporate a more holistic view of employee well-being.

Considerations:

This includes not only financial aspects like salary and bonuses but also physical health, mental well-being, and work-life balance. Comprehensive well-being programs may become integral to compensation packages.

2. Personalization and Customization:

Prediction:

The trend toward personalized and customizable benefits will intensify.

Considerations:

Employees will seek greater flexibility in tailoring their compensation packages to align with individual needs. This may involve a menu of benefits from which employees can choose, such as healthcare options, flexible work arrangements, and unique perks.

3. Increased Transparency and Communication:

Prediction:

Organizations will continue to move towards greater transparency in communicating compensation structures.

Considerations:

Employees will demand clearer communication about how salaries are determined, the impact of performance on compensation, and how organizations position themselves in terms of pay equity.

4. Integration of Technology:

Prediction:

Technology will play a more significant role in salary systems.

Considerations:

Artificial intelligence and data analytics will be used for more accurate market benchmarking, personalized compensation recommendations, and real-time performance tracking. Technology may also facilitate more seamless and transparent compensation processes.

5. Focus on Equity and Inclusion:

Prediction:

There will be a continued emphasis on achieving equity in compensation.

Considerations:

Organizations will proactively address gender pay gaps, diversity, and inclusion. This may involve regular audits, transparent reporting, and initiatives to ensure fair compensation practices for all employees.

6. Shift in Performance Metrics:

Prediction:

Performance metrics will evolve to capture a broader view of employee contributions.

Considerations:

Companies may move away from traditional performance reviews and explore more continuous feedback models. Metrics could include collaboration, innovation, and adaptability, reflecting the changing nature of work.

7. Rise of Gig Economy and Flexible Work:

Prediction:

Compensation systems will adapt to the growing gig economy and increased demand for flexible work arrangements.

Considerations:

Companies may develop innovative payment structures for gig workers, freelancers, and part-time employees. The value of flexibility may be reflected in compensation, and organizations may offer more dynamic payment models.

8. Impact of Remote and Hybrid Work:

Prediction:

The remote and hybrid work trends will influence how compensation is structured.

Considerations:

Companies may reconsider geographic-based pay structures, moving towards more standardized or skills-based compensation. Remote work allowances and home office support may become integral components of compensation packages.

9. Government Regulations and Social Movements:

Prediction:

Governments and social movements will continue to influence compensation practices.

Considerations:

Regulations around pay equity, minimum wages, and transparency may evolve. Social movements advocating for fair and ethical compensation will drive changes in organizational practices.

10. Continued Evolution of Benefits:

Prediction:

Employee benefits will undergo continuous evolution.

Considerations:

Beyond traditional benefits, organizations may introduce new perks related to mental health support, family care, continuous learning, and financial wellness.

While predicting the future of salary systems involves some uncertainty, these insights and considerations provide a glimpse into potential trends. Organizations that remain agile, responsive to employee needs, and aligned with broader societal shifts will be better positioned to navigate the evolving landscape of compensation practices. The key will be striking a balance between competitive pay and benefits, transparency, and a strong focus on employee well-being and equity.

Technological impact:

How technology might impact compensation practices. – Let us discuss the potential impact of technology on the future of salary systems.

Technological Impact: Revolutionizing Compensation Practices

In the ever-evolving landscape of the modern workplace, technology stands as a transformative force, reshaping various facets of business operations. One area where technology is making significant inroads is in the realm of compensation practices. From innovative tools that aid in data analytics to the use of artificial intelligence (AI) for personalized compensation packages, the technological impact on the future of salary systems is profound and multifaceted.

1. Data-Driven Decision-Making:

One of the primary ways technology is influencing compensation practices is through data-driven decision-making. HR departments now leverage advanced analytics tools to gather and analyze data related to employee performance, market salary trends, and overall workforce dynamics. These insights enable organizations to make informed decisions about salary structures, ensuring they remain competitive in the talent market.

Data analytics is emerging as a powerful tool for HR professionals in shaping compensation strategies. By analyzing large datasets, organizations can gain insights into market trends, employee performance, and workforce dynamics. This data-driven approach allows for more accurate market benchmarking, enabling organizations to set competitive and fair salary structures.

Example:

Companies can use data analytics to compare their compensation packages with industry benchmarks, identify pay gaps, and adjust salaries to attract and retain top talent.

2. Artificial Intelligence in Compensation Planning:

The advent of AI has ushered in a new era of precision and personalization in compensation planning. AI algorithms can process vast amounts of data to tailor compensation packages based on individual employee contributions, skills, and market value. This personalized approach goes beyond traditional one-size-fits-all models, allowing organizations to optimize their compensation strategies.

a) AI and Data Analytics in Compensation:

Automation of HR Processes:

As artificial intelligence (AI) and machine learning become more sophisticated, HR processes are undergoing automation. This includes tasks related to compensation, such as payroll processing, performance evaluations, and benefits administration. Automation not only increases efficiency but also reduces the margin of error in compensation-related tasks.

b) personalized Compensation Packages:

AI can facilitate the creation of personalized compensation packages. By considering individual skills, performance metrics, and career trajectories, AI algorithms can recommend customized benefits and bonuses. This personalized approach not only caters to the unique needs of employees but also fosters a sense of value and recognition.

c) AI-Enhanced Recruitment and Compensation Benchmarking:

Smarter Hiring Decisions:

AI-driven recruitment tools contribute to more informed hiring decisions. By analysing candidate data and market trends, AI can help organizations determine the appropriate compensation for new hires based on skills, experience, and industry benchmarks. This ensures that salary offers align with both organizational standards and external market conditions.

d) Real-Time Compensation Benchmarking:

Traditional compensation benchmarking processes can be time-consuming and lag behind market changes. AI-powered tools enable real-time benchmarking by continuously monitoring industry trends and salary data. This agility allows organizations to adjust compensation strategies promptly to remain competitive.

Example:

AI algorithms can analyze an employee's performance, experience, and industry demand to recommend a customized compensation package, including salary, bonuses, and benefits.

3. Predictive Analytics for Retention Strategies:

Technology enables the use of predictive analytics to identify patterns and trends that can inform retention strategies. By analyzing factors such as employee engagement, job satisfaction, and compensation levels, organizations can predict potential attrition risks and take proactive measures to retain valuable talent.

a) Predictive Analytics for Workforce Planning:

Anticipating Compensation Needs:

Predictive analytics tools use historical data and algorithms to forecast future trends. In the context of compensation, organizations can use predictive analytics for workforce planning. This includes anticipating talent shortages, identifying critical skill gaps, and proactively adjusting compensation strategies to attract and retain key talent.

b) Scenario Modelling:

Advanced analytics enables scenario modelling for compensation planning. Organizations can simulate the impact of different economic conditions, market trends, or policy changes on their compensation budgets. This proactive approach helps organizations stay agile in responding to external factors that may influence salary systems.

Example:

Predictive analytics can alert HR teams about employees who may be at risk of leaving due to salary misalignment. The organization can then initiate conversations about adjustments to retain these individuals.

4. Blockchain for Transparent Compensation:

Blockchain technology works by creating a decentralized and immutable ledger of transactions, which is maintained by a network of computers (nodes) rather than a single centralized authority. Here's a simplified explanation of how blockchain works in the context of a salary system:

a) Transaction Creation:

When an employer initiates a salary payment to an employee, this transaction is recorded as a block on the blockchain. The transaction includes details such as the employee's identity, the amount of salary, and any other relevant information.

b) Validation:

Before a block is added to the blockchain, it must be validated by the network of nodes. These nodes use complex algorithms to verify the transaction's validity, ensuring that the sender has the necessary funds and that the transaction meets predefined criteria.

c) Block Addition:

Once validated, the block is added to the blockchain, forming a chronological chain of transactions. Each block contains a unique cryptographic hash that links it to the previous block, creating an immutable record of transactions.

d) Decentralization:

The blockchain is distributed across the network of nodes, with each node maintaining a copy of the entire ledger. This decentralization ensures that no single entity has control over the blockchain, making it resistant to tampering or manipulation.

e) Consensus Mechanisms:

Blockchain networks use consensus mechanisms to agree on the validity of transactions and the addition of new blocks to the chain. Common consensus mechanisms include Proof of Work (PoW), Proof of Stake (PoS), and Delegated Proof of Stake (DPoS).

f) Smart Contracts:

In addition to recording transactions, blockchain platforms like Ethereum allow for the creation and execution of smart contracts. These self-executing contracts automatically enforce predefined conditions when certain criteria are met, such as releasing salary payments to employees on a specified date.

g) Security:

Blockchain technology employs advanced cryptographic techniques to secure transactions and prevent unauthorized access. Each block is cryptographically linked to the previous block, forming a tamper-proof chain. Additionally, the decentralized nature of blockchain makes it resilient to single points of failure or attack.

Overall, blockchain technology provides a transparent, secure, and efficient means of recording and managing salary payments in a decentralized manner.

By leveraging blockchain, organizations can enhance trust, reduce administrative overhead, and streamline salary processes for employees and employers alike.

Blockchain technology is gaining traction in ensuring transparency and security in compensation practices. By utilizing blockchain for salary records, organizations can create an immutable and transparent ledger, providing employees with verifiable proof of their compensation history. This not only enhances trust but also simplifies compliance and auditing processes.

Blockchain and Transparent Payroll:

a) Securing Payroll Transactions:

Blockchain technology has the potential to enhance the security and transparency of payroll transactions. By creating decentralized and tamper-resistant ledgers, blockchain can ensure the integrity of payroll data, reducing the risk of errors or fraudulent activities in compensation processes.

b) Smart Contracts for Compensation Agreements:

Smart contracts, powered by blockchain, can automate compensation agreements. These self-executing contracts can trigger payments based on predefined conditions, such as reaching performance milestones or completing specific projects. This not only streamlines the compensation process but also adds a layer of trust.

Example:

An employee can access a secure and transparent blockchain record that details their entire compensation history, including salary adjustments, bonuses, and stock options.

5. Employee Self-Service Platforms:

Technology has empowered employees through self-service platforms where they can access and manage their compensation information in real time. These platforms provide transparency and autonomy, allowing employees to view their total compensation, benefits, and performance metrics at their convenience.

Employee Experience Platforms: Enhancing Employee Engagement

Employee experience platforms leverage technology to enhance overall employee engagement, including compensation-related experiences. These platforms often provide personalized dashboards where employees can access information about their compensation, benefits, and performance metrics. This contributes to a positive employee experience and improves communication around compensation matters.

Real-Time Communication:
Digital platforms facilitate real-time communication between employees and HR teams. This is particularly valuable for addressing compensation-related queries and concerns promptly. Employees can receive instant updates on salary adjustments, bonuses, and benefits through these platforms.

Example:

An employee can log into a self-service portal to view their current salary, bonuses, and benefits, as well as simulate the impact of performance improvements on future compensation.

6. Virtual and Augmented Reality in Training:

Technological advancements like virtual and augmented reality are enhancing training and development programs, influencing compensation indirectly. By providing immersive learning experiences, organizations can upskill employees, making them more valuable and potentially justifying higher compensation.

Example:

An employee participating in a virtual reality training program for advanced technical skills may become eligible for a higher salary upon successful completion.

7. Continuous Feedback Apps:

Technology is facilitating a shift from traditional annual performance reviews to continuous feedback models. Mobile apps and online platforms enable real-time feedback, allowing managers to provide instant recognition and address performance concerns promptly. This can have a direct impact on compensation decisions tied to performance.

Example:

A manager using a continuous feedback app can acknowledge an employee's exceptional performance immediately, triggering a timelier compensation review.

8. Skill-Based Pay Models:

As technology continues to disrupt industries, the demand for specific skills evolves rapidly. Skill-based pay models, enabled by technology, allow organizations to adjust compensation based on the relevance and scarcity of particular skills in the job market.

Example:

An employee acquiring a certification in a high-demand technology skill may see an immediate increase in their compensation, reflecting the added value to the organization.

9. Automation and Job Evolution:

Automation and artificial intelligence are transforming job roles, creating new opportunities and challenges. Organizations are adopting a more dynamic approach to compensation as roles evolve. Technology enables a swift response to changes in job responsibilities and market demand.

Example:

An employee whose role evolves with the introduction of automation may receive additional training and compensation adjustments, aligning with the increased complexity of their responsibilities.

10. Mobile-Based Benefits and Rewards:

Mobile technology is reshaping how organizations communicate and deliver benefits and rewards to employees. Mobile apps provide a convenient way for employees to access information about bonuses, benefits, and other incentives, fostering engagement and satisfaction.

Example:

An employee receives a notification on their mobile app about a performance bonus being credited to their account, enhancing the immediacy and impact of the reward.

Challenges and Considerations:

While the technological impact on compensation practices is transformative, there are challenges and considerations that organizations must address:

1. Data Privacy and Security:

With increased reliance on data analytics and AI, ensuring the privacy and security of employee information becomes paramount.

Cybersecurity and Privacy Considerations:

Protecting Sensitive Compensation Data.

With the increased reliance on technology comes a heightened need for robust cybersecurity measures. Protecting sensitive compensation data from cyber threats is imperative. Organizations must invest in secure systems, encryption protocols, and employee training to safeguard confidential salary information.

Ensuring Data Privacy Compliance:

As technology facilitates the collection and analysis of vast amounts of employee data, organizations must prioritize compliance with data privacy regulations. Implementing transparent policies and ensuring that compensation practices adhere to privacy laws are crucial considerations.

2. **Equity and Bias:**

AI algorithms may inadvertently perpetuate biases if not carefully designed. Organizations must continually assess and adjust algorithms to ensure fairness in compensation decisions.

3. **Employee Adoption:**

The successful implementation of technology in compensation practices relies on employee acceptance and understanding. Organizations should invest in comprehensive communication and training programs.

4. **Regulatory Compliance:**

As technology introduces new ways of handling compensation, organizations must stay abreast of evolving regulations to maintain compliance.

5. **Performance Tracking and Feedback.**

Continuous Performance Monitoring:

Technology enables real-time performance tracking, moving beyond traditional annual reviews. Continuous performance monitoring tools allow managers to provide timely feedback, assess contributions, and align compensation adjustments with ongoing achievements. This dynamic feedback loop contributes to a more agile and responsive compensation system.

6. Objective Metrics and Transparency:

Technology facilitates the use of objective metrics in performance assessments. Transparent and quantifiable metrics, often facilitated by digital platforms, reduce biases and enhance fairness in compensation decisions. Employees can have a clearer understanding of how their performance contributes to salary adjustments.

7. Remote Work and Digital Nomadism.

Decoupling Salary from Location:

The rise of remote work, accelerated by technological advancements, challenges the traditional link between compensation and geographic location. Organizations are exploring ways to decouple salaries from physical office locations. Technology facilitates virtual collaboration and communication, enabling companies to tap into a global talent pool without being constrained by regional salary norms.

Digital Nomadism and Compensation Flexibility:

Digital nomadism refers to a lifestyle where individuals use technology to work remotely and live a location-independent lifestyle. Digital nomads typically rely on the internet to perform their jobs, allowing them to work from anywhere with an internet connection. They often travel frequently, choosing to live in different cities or countries for short to extended periods while maintaining their remote work arrangements. This lifestyle provides flexibility and freedom, allowing individuals to explore new places while continuing to pursue their careers or businesses.

With the emergence of digital nomadism, employees are increasingly seeking flexibility in work arrangements. Technology allows organizations to adopt more flexible compensation models, accommodating diverse preferences.

Compensation packages can be tailored to support remote work, including allowances for home office setups and considerations for the cost of living in different regions.

As we stand on the precipice of a technological revolution, various industries are undergoing transformative changes, and the realm of human resources and compensation practices is no exception. The integration of technology is reshaping how organizations attract, retain, and reward talent. This comprehensive exploration delves into the potential impact of technology on the future of salary systems, encompassing artificial intelligence, data analytics, automation, and the broader digital landscape.

Conclusion

Navigating the Future Landscape:

The integration of technology into compensation practices represents a paradigm shift in organizations manage their workforce. The future of salary systems will be characterized by agility, personalization, transparency, and seamless integration of ever-evolving technology.

The technological impact on the future of salary systems is dynamic and promising. From data-driven decision-making to the use of AI for personalized compensation, organizations are leveraging technology to create more agile, transparent, and employee-centric compensation practices. Embracing these technological advancements is not just about staying competitive; it's about fostering a culture of continuous improvement and adaptability in the rapidly changing world of work. As organizations navigate these advancements, the key will be to strike a balance between leveraging technology for efficiency and maintaining the human touch in compensation practices.

"Compensation is more than just a pay-check; it's a reflection of value and commitment."

Chapter 11

Employee Engagement and Retention

In this chapter, we delve into the pivotal role of employee engagement and retention in fostering organizational success. Beyond mere job satisfaction lies a deeper connection between employees and their work, one that fuels productivity, innovation, and loyalty. Join us as we explore strategies to cultivate a culture of engagement, where employees feel valued, empowered, and motivated to contribute their best. From nurturing strong leadership to fostering open communication and recognition, we uncover the key drivers of employee engagement and retention. Discover how organizations can create an environment where talent thrives and turnover becomes a thing of the past.

Let us discuss on how compensation contributes to employee satisfaction and retention.

The Role of Compensation in Employee Satisfaction and Retention

Compensation is a critical component of the overall employment experience and plays a pivotal role in shaping employee satisfaction and retention. It goes beyond the mere transactional aspect of a paychecks, encompassing various elements such as salary, bonuses, benefits, and non-monetary perks.

Here's an exploration of how compensation contributes to employee satisfaction and retention:

1. Attracting Top Talent:

Contribution:

Competitive compensation packages are instrumental in attracting top talent to an organization.

Effect:

Prospective employees often compare job offers based on the overall compensation offered, and organizations offering competitive salaries and benefits are more likely to attract and secure high-calibre candidates.

2. Recognition of Value:

Contribution:

Compensation serves as a tangible acknowledgement of an employee's value to the organization.

Effect:

When employees feel that their contributions are recognized and appropriately compensated, it fosters a sense of worth and accomplishment, leading to higher job satisfaction.

3. Motivation and Performance:

Contribution:

Compensation, including performance-related bonuses and incentives, serves as a motivational tool.

Effect:

Employees who see a direct correlation between their efforts, achievements, and financial rewards are likely to be more motivated, leading to increased job satisfaction and better performance.

4. Retention:

Contribution:

Competitive compensation is a key factor in retaining talent, and preventing employee turnover.

Effect:

When employees are satisfied with their compensation, they are less likely to seek alternative employment opportunities, contributing to higher retention rates and stability within the organization.

5. Financial Well-being:

Contribution:

Compensation directly impacts the financial well-being of employees.

Effect:

Employees who feel financially secure due to a competitive salary and comprehensive benefits are more likely to experience reduced stress, leading to increased overall job satisfaction and better mental health.

6. Perceived Fairness:

Contribution:

The perceived fairness of compensation structures is crucial for employee satisfaction.

Effect:

When employees believe that compensation is fair and equitable, it fosters a positive work environment, enhances morale, and contributes to a culture of trust and transparency.

7. Employee Engagement:

Contribution:

Compensation influences the level of engagement employees have with their work.

Effect:

Well-compensated employees are more likely to be engaged in their roles, leading to higher productivity, a positive work atmosphere, and increased job satisfaction.

8. Career Progression:

Contribution:

Compensation structures often include opportunities for career progression and development.

Effect:

When employees see a clear path for advancement and associated financial rewards, it not only contributes to job satisfaction but also enhances retention as individuals are more likely to stay with an organization that invests in their career growth.

9. Market Competitiveness:

Contribution:

Ensuring that compensation is competitive within the industry is essential.

Effect:

If employees believe they can receive better compensation elsewhere, they may be more inclined to explore external opportunities. Therefore, maintaining market competitiveness is crucial for employee satisfaction and retention.

10. Alignment with Values:

Contribution:

Compensation practices should align with an organization's values and culture.

Effect:

Employees are more likely to be satisfied and stay with an organization that values their well-being and aligns with their personal and professional values.

Challenges and Considerations:

While compensation is a significant factor in employee satisfaction and retention, there are challenges and considerations organizations must navigate:

1. Equity and Fairness:

Ensuring fairness and equity in compensation structures to avoid disparities that may lead to dissatisfaction and turnover.

2. Communication:

Transparent communication about compensation structures and changes is crucial for maintaining employee trust and satisfaction.

3. Non-Monetary Factors:

While compensation is vital, other factors such as work-life balance, a positive work culture, and opportunities for professional development also play pivotal roles in employee satisfaction.

4. Individual Preferences:

Employee satisfaction is subjective, and individual preferences may vary. Organizations need to recognize and accommodate diverse needs.

Compensation is a linchpin in the complex web of factors that contribute to employee satisfaction and retention. It is not only a reflection of an employee's value to the organization but also a powerful tool for motivation, engagement, and overall well-being. As organizations navigate the intricacies of compensation, they must consider the holistic needs of their workforce, align compensation practices with organizational values, and continually assess and adapt their approaches to ensure employee satisfaction and retention in an ever-evolving workplace landscape.

Retention Strategies:

Leveraging Compensation to Retain Top Talent

In the competitive landscape of today's job market, retaining top talent is a key challenge for organizations. Compensation plays a pivotal role in employee retention, and strategic approaches to compensation can significantly impact an organization's ability to keep its best performers.

Here are effective strategies for using compensation to retain top talent:

1. Competitive Salaries:

Strategy:

Ensure that your organization offers competitive base salaries that align with industry standards.

Impact:

Competitive salaries signal to top talent that they are valued and that their contributions are recognized, making them less likely to explore opportunities with competitors.

2. Performance-Based Bonuses:

Strategy:

Implement a robust performance bonus system tied to individual and team achievements.

Impact:

Performance-based bonuses provide tangible recognition for exceptional contributions, motivating top talent to consistently deliver high-quality results.

3. Profit Sharing and Stock Options:

Strategy:

Introduce profit-sharing programs or offer stock options to align employees with the company's long-term success.

Impact:

By linking compensation to the organization's financial performance, employees have a vested interest in the company's growth, fostering loyalty and commitment.

4. Retention Bonuses:

Strategy:

Provide retention bonuses to key employees at critical junctures, such as after a significant project completion or during periods of organizational change.

Impact:

Retention bonuses demonstrate a commitment to retaining valuable talent during pivotal moments, mitigating the risk of key individuals leaving.

5. Customizable Benefits Packages:

Strategy:

Offer flexible and customizable benefits packages that allow employees to tailor their compensation to meet their unique needs.

Impact:

Customizable benefits enhance job satisfaction by addressing individual preferences and life circumstances, making employees more likely to stay with the organization.

6. Career Development Opportunities:

Strategy:

Tie compensation increases to career progression and development milestones.

Impact:

Employees are more likely to stay if they see a clear path for advancement within the organization, with associated compensation benefits as they climb the career ladder.

7. Educational Assistance Programs:

Strategy:

Provide financial support for ongoing education and skill development.

Impact:

Investing in employees' continued education not only enhances their skill set but also fosters a sense of loyalty as they recognize the organization's commitment to their professional growth.

8. Recognition and Appreciation Programs:

Strategy:

Implement programs that recognize and appreciate outstanding performance.

Impact:

Regular recognition, whether through monetary rewards or public acknowledgement, reinforces the value placed on employees, enhancing job satisfaction and reducing turnover.

9. Transparent Compensation Policies:

Strategy:

Maintain transparency in compensation policies and communicate clearly about how salaries are determined.

Impact:

Transparent communication builds trust, reducing the likelihood that employees will leave due to perceived inequities or lack of clarity about their compensation.

10. Employee Well-being Initiatives:

Strategy:

Introduce well-being initiatives such as health and wellness programs, mental health support, and flexible work arrangements.

Impact:

An organization that prioritizes employee well-being through compensation-related initiatives is likely to have a more satisfied and committed workforce.

11. Benchmarking and Market Analysis:

Strategy:

Regularly conduct benchmarking and market analysis to ensure that your compensation packages remain competitive.

Impact:

Staying informed about industry standards enables organizations to adjust their compensation strategies proactively, preventing top talent from being lured away by more lucrative offers.

12. Exit Interviews and Feedback:

Strategy:

Conduct thorough exit interviews to understand the reasons behind employee departures.

Impact:

Insights from exit interviews can inform adjustments to compensation strategies, addressing issues and concerns that may be contributing to turnover.

13. Regular Compensation Reviews:

Strategy:

Conduct regular reviews of compensation structures to ensure they align with the organization's goals and industry trends.

Impact:

Proactive reviews allow organizations to identify and address any disparities, ensuring that compensation remains a compelling factor for retaining top talent.

14. Retention Analytics:

Strategy:

Utilize analytics to identify flight risks and predict potential turnover.

Impact:

Predictive analytics can help organizations take pre-emptive measures to retain top talent by addressing issues before they escalate.

15. Continuous Communication:

Strategy:

Foster open communication about compensation, benefits, and overall employee satisfaction.

Impact:

Regular discussions about compensation and its connection to performance and organizational goals create an environment of transparency, trust, and engagement.

Conclusion

Using compensation strategically to retain top talent requires a comprehensive approach that goes beyond just competitive salaries. By combining financial rewards with recognition, career development opportunities, and a commitment to employee well-being, organizations can create a compelling and holistic compensation package. Regularly reassessing and adapting these strategies ensures that compensation remains a powerful tool in the arsenal of employee retention efforts. Ultimately, a well-thought-out compensation strategy sends a clear message to top talent: their contributions are valued, recognized, and rewarded, making them more likely to choose long-term commitment to the organization.

"Competitive compensation attracts top talent, but a supportive work culture retains them."

Chapter 12

Communication about Compensation

Welcome to a chapter dedicated to the art of transparent communication about compensation. In this digital age, where information flows freely, employees seek clarity and openness regarding their compensation packages. Join us as we embark on a journey to demystify the complexities of salary structures, benefits, and incentives. We delve into the importance of clear, honest communication between employers and employees, fostering trust and alignment of expectations. From effective salary discussions to transparent policies and practices, we explore how organizations can foster a culture of openness and fairness in compensation communication. Prepare to empower your workforce with knowledge and transparency, laying the foundation for mutual understanding and satisfaction.

Let us know about thc Importancc of Transparent Communication in Salary Decisions.

Transparent communication about salary decisions is a cornerstone of a healthy and thriving workplace. It involves openly sharing information about how compensation is determined, the factors considered, and the organization's overall approach to rewarding its employees. Emphasizing transparency in salary communication has profound effects on employee morale, trust, and overall organizational success.

Here's a closer look at why transparent communication about salary decisions is crucial:

1. Fosters Trust and Credibility:

Importance:

Transparency builds trust, a fundamental element of any successful employer-employee relationship.

Effect:

When employees understand how salary decisions are made and believe in the fairness of the process, it fosters a sense of credibility in the organization's leadership.

2. Addresses Perceived Inequities:

Importance:

Lack of transparency can lead to perceived inequities among employees.

Effect:

Transparent communication helps address misconceptions and ensures that employees are aware of the factors considered in determining compensation, reducing the likelihood of resentment or dissatisfaction.

3. Aligns Expectations:

Importance:

Transparent communication sets clear expectations regarding compensation.

Effect:

Employees who have a realistic understanding of how their performance and contributions impact their compensation are more likely to align their expectations with organizational goals, reducing potential disappointment or frustration.

4. Enhances Job Satisfaction:

Importance:

Understanding the connection between performance and compensation contributes to job satisfaction.

Effect:

Employees who feel that their efforts are acknowledged and rewarded appropriately are more likely to be satisfied in their roles, leading to increased motivation and productivity.

5. Supports Employee Engagement:

Importance:

Transparent communication fosters a culture of openness and inclusivity.

Effect:

Engaged employees are more likely to contribute positively to the organization. Transparency in salary decisions contributes to an inclusive culture, encouraging employees to actively participate in their roles and the organization's success.

6. Mitigates Employee Turnover:

Importance:

A lack of transparency can contribute to employee turnover.

Effect:

Employees may seek opportunities elsewhere if they perceive unfairness in compensation decisions. Transparent communication can mitigate turnover by addressing concerns and demonstrating the organization's commitment to fairness.

7. Encourages Salary Discussions:

Importance:

Transparent communication promotes open discussions about compensation.

Effect:

Employees are more likely to feel comfortable discussing their compensation when they understand the process. This allows for constructive conversations, enabling organizations to address concerns and make adjustments where necessary.

8. Demonstrates Organizational Values:

Importance:

Transparent communication reflects an organization's commitment to its values.

Effect:

When an organization openly communicates about salary decisions, it signals a commitment to fairness, equity, and valuing its employees. This aligns with organizational values and contributes to a positive corporate culture.

9. Empowers Employees:

Importance:

Understanding the factors that influence compensation empowers employees to take control of their professional development.

Effect:

When employees know how to enhance their skills or performance to positively impact their compensation, it creates a sense of ownership and empowerment, leading to increased job satisfaction.

10. Addresses Diversity and Inclusion:

Importance:

Transparent communication supports diversity and inclusion initiatives.

Effect:

By openly discussing compensation decisions, organizations can identify and address any potential biases in their processes, fostering an inclusive workplace where all employees feel valued and respected.

11. Meets Legal and Regulatory Standards:

Importance:

Transparency aligns with legal and regulatory requirements related to compensation disclosure.

Effect:

Complying with transparency standards ensures that organizations meet legal obligations and fosters a culture of accountability and responsibility.

12. Improves Employee Performance:

Importance:

Transparent communication helps employees understand the link between performance and rewards.

Effect:

Employees who know how their contributions impact their compensation are more likely to be motivated to excel in their roles, leading to improved overall organizational performance.

Transparent communication about salary decisions is not merely a nice-to-have aspect of organizational culture; it is a critical element that underpins trust, engagement, and satisfaction among employees. Organizations that prioritize open communication regarding compensation demonstrate a commitment to fairness, equity, and employee well-being. This, in turn, contributes to a positive work environment, enhances organizational reputation, and positions the company as an employer of choice. By recognizing the importance of transparency in salary communication, organizations can build stronger, more resilient teams and drive sustained success.

Effectively communicating changes in compensation is crucial for employers to maintain trust and morale among their workforce.

Here are some tips for employers to ensure that these communications are handled sensitively and effectively:

1. Prepare Thoroughly

Understand the Details:

Be clear about what the changes are, why they are being made, and how they will impact employees.

Anticipate Questions:

Prepare answers for potential questions employees might have regarding the changes.

2. Be Transparent

Share the Reasoning:

Clearly explain the reasons behind the changes. Whether it's due to economic factors, company performance, or a change in compensation strategy, being honest helps build trust.

Discuss the Process:

Outline how decisions were made, including any factors or data considered.

3. Communicate Early and Often

Avoid Surprises:

Communicate changes as early as possible. Avoid letting employees hear about them through rumours or third parties.

Regular Updates:

If the change is being implemented over time, provide regular updates to keep employees informed about the progress and what to expect next.

4. Use Clear and Simple Language

Avoid Jargon:

Use straightforward language to ensure that all employees, regardless of their position or background, can understand the changes.

Be Concise:

Deliver the information in a concise, easy-to-understand manner.

5. Ensure Consistent Messaging

Unified Voice:

Make sure that all managers and HR representatives are on the same page and communicating the same message.

Written Documentation:

Provide written documentation (like emails or memos) to supplement verbal communication for clarity and reference.

6. Personalize the Communication

Individual Impact:

Explain to employees how the changes will specifically affect them.

One-on-One Meetings:

Offer individual meetings to discuss personal concerns and provide clarity.

7. Provide a Platform for Feedback

Encourage Dialogue:

Allow employees to ask questions and express concerns. This can be through meetings, suggestion boxes, or anonymous surveys.

Actively Listen:

Show that the company values their opinions and is willing to address concerns.

8. Highlight the Positives

Focus on Benefits:

If there are positive aspects of the change, such as improved long-term stability or new opportunities for bonuses, highlight these.

Future Prospects:

Discuss how the changes align with the company's future goals and how they can benefit employees in the long run.

9. Offer Support

Resources:

Provide resources such as FAQs, financial counselling, or workshops, especially if the changes might negatively impact some employees.

HR Availability:

Ensure HR is available and prepared to offer support and answer questions.

10. Follow-Up

Check-In:

After the announcement, check in with employees to gauge their reaction and address any lingering concerns.

Monitor Morale:

Keep an eye on the overall company morale and be ready to make adjustments or provide additional support where necessary.

11. Maintain Sensitivity

Empathy:

Acknowledge that changes might be difficult for some employees and approach the communication with empathy and understanding.

Respect Concerns:

Treat all employee concerns with respect, even if they can't be immediately addressed.

Conclusion

Communication about compensation changes is a delicate process that needs to be handled with care and planning. By being transparent, empathetic, and proactive in their communication strategy, employers can help ensure that these changes are received as positively as possible and maintain a strong, trusting relationship with their workforce.

"A well-compensated workforce is a powerful asset for achieving corporate goals."

Chapter 13

Resources and Tools

In this chapter, we provide you with an arsenal of resources and tools to navigate the intricate landscape of compensation management. From salary calculators to industry benchmarks, we offer practical solutions to help you make informed decisions and optimize your compensation strategies. Dive into a wealth of online resources, including salary surveys, compensation software, and best practice guides. Explore case studies and success stories from leading organizations, showcasing innovative approaches to compensation management. Whether you're a seasoned HR professional or a budding entrepreneur, these resources and tools are designed to empower you on your journey towards compensation excellence. Get ready to harness the power of data, technology, and expertise to elevate your compensation practices to new heights.

Here in this chapter information is given on “Resources and Tools," focusing on recommended software and tools for effective payroll and compensation management:

1. Payroll Processing Software:

ADP Workforce Now:

A comprehensive payroll and HR solution that handles tax compliance, benefits administration, and time and attendance tracking.

Gusto:

A user-friendly platform offering payroll services, benefits administration, and compliance support, suitable for small to medium-sized businesses.

Paychex Flex:

Provides payroll processing, HR, and benefits administration services, catering to businesses of various sizes.

Wave:

An accounting and payroll solution suitable for small businesses and freelancers, offering a free accounting and invoicing platform.

QuickBooks Online:

Provides cloud-based accounting and payroll services, scalable for businesses of various sizes.

Payroll4Free:

A free payroll processing service suitable for small businesses, offering basic payroll features.

2. Compensation Management Software:

CompTrak:

A cloud-based compensation management platform that assists in designing, managing, and optimizing compensation plans. Offers global compensation management solutions, taking into account currency variations and local regulations.

Salary.com:

Offers a range of compensation data and software solutions to help organizations make informed decisions about employee pay.

BambooHR:

While primarily an HR software, BambooHR includes features for tracking employee compensation, benefits, and performance. While widely used in the United States, BambooHR has users globally and can be adapted for international HR and compensation management needs.

ZohoPeople:

A cloud-based HRIS that supports global HR and compensation management.

3. HRIS (Human Resources Information System):

Workday:

An all-in-one HRIS that includes features for payroll, workforce planning, and compensation management.

Oracle Cloud HCM:

Integrates HR, payroll, and talent management, providing a unified platform for managing human resources.

SAP Success Factors:

A cloud-based HRIS that covers various HR functions, including compensation and benefits.

BambooHR:

As mentioned earlier, BambooHR provides global HR functionality.

ZohoPeople:

Offers a comprehensive HRIS solution with global capabilities, allowing organizations to manage employees across different countries.

PeopleSoft (Oracle):

An enterprise-level HRIS that supports global HR and payroll operations.

4. Benefits Administration Software:

Zenefits:

A platform that combines HR, benefits administration, payroll, and compliance in one integrated solution. While focused on the U.S., Zenefits can be adapted for global benefits administration with features like time tracking and leave management.

BambooHR:

Apart from compensation management, BambooHR includes features for benefits administration. It can be used for global benefits administration and integrates with various third-party tools.

BerniePortal:

Designed for benefits brokers, BerniePortal helps manage benefits, payroll, and compliance. Tailored for benefits brokers, BerniePortal can handle benefits administration for a global workforce.

5. Performance Management Software:

15Five:

A performance management platform that facilitates continuous feedback, goal tracking, and performance reviews. Suitable for global teams, 15Five focuses on fostering continuous employee feedback and goal tracking.

Lattice:

Provides tools for performance reviews, goal setting, and employee engagement. Offers performance management tools suitable for global teams with features like goal setting and continuous feedback.

Workday:

Integrates performance management with other HR functions, allowing for a holistic approach to employee development. Known for its scalability, Workday can handle performance management for large, multinational organizations.

6. Employee Communication Tools:

Slack:

Widely used globally for team communication, Slack offers multi-language support, making it accessible for diverse teams. An instant messaging platform that facilitates communication within teams, promoting transparency.

Microsoft Teams:

With its integration capabilities and diverse communication features, Teams is suitable for global collaboration. Combines chat, video conferencing, file storage, and application integration for effective team collaboration.

Asana or Trello:

Project management tools that help teams organize and track work, enhancing overall communication.

WhatsApp:

Widely used globally for instant messaging, especially in regions with a strong presence of mobile users.

7. Legal and Compliance Resources:

Department of Labor (DOL) Website:

Provides information on federal labour laws, wage and hour regulations, and compliance resources.

Society for Human Resource Management (SHRM):

Offers resources and articles on HR best practices, including compliance and legal updates.

Local Labor Departments:

Depending on the jurisdiction, accessing state or regional labour department websites can provide information on specific regulations and compliance requirements.

International Labor Organization (ILO):

Offers global labour standards and information on labour laws worldwide.

Global HR Compliance:

Provides resources and tools for HR professionals to stay compliant with labour laws globally.

Local Government Websites:

For specific countries, accessing government labour department websites can provide insights into local regulations.

Remember to choose tools that align with the size and needs of the organization. Additionally, stay informed about updates and new features offered by these tools, as the field of HR and payroll management is continuously evolving. Always verify the suitability of a tool for your specific requirements before implementation.

Conclusion

When selecting tools for global use, consider factors such as multi-language support, compliance with diverse regulatory environments, and adaptability to local currencies and tax structures. Additionally, keep in mind that in some regions, cloud-based solutions may be preferred due to accessibility challenges associated with on-premise software. Always verify the compatibility of a tool with local regulations and ensure that it meets the specific needs of your global workforce.

"Happy employees are the best currency of any successful business."

Chapter 14

Considerations for New Entrepreneurs in Workforce Selection

Embarking on the journey of entrepreneurship requires careful consideration and strategic planning, especially when it comes to building your team. In this chapter, we delve into the essential considerations for new entrepreneurs in selecting the right workforce for their ventures. From defining your hiring needs to crafting job descriptions, we guide you through the initial stages of workforce planning. Explore innovative recruitment strategies, including leveraging social media platforms and networking events to attract top talent. Learn how to conduct effective interviews and assessments to identify candidates who align with your company culture and values. We also address the importance of diversity and inclusion in building a dynamic and resilient team. Whether you're a solo entrepreneur or leading a start-up team, this chapter equips you with the knowledge and tools to make informed decisions in workforce selection and lay the foundation for your business success.

Points to be considered by a new entrepreneur, company, or organization while selecting manpower or employees for their businesses:

When a new entrepreneur, company, or organization is in the process of selecting manpower or employees, several crucial points must be considered, especially since they will be investing in their salaries and well-being. These considerations are key to building a strong foundation for the business with a capable and effective workforce.

Here's a detailed guide:

1. Skillset and Expertise:

Focus:

Identify the specific skills and expertise required for each role.

Consideration:

Look for candidates with a balance of technical skills and industry knowledge pertinent to your business needs.

2. Cultural Fit:

Focus:

Assess how well a candidate aligns with the company's culture, values, and vision.

Consideration:

Hire individuals who not only have the right skills but also resonate with the company's ethos and work environment.

3. Adaptability and Growth Potential:

Focus:

Evaluate the candidate's ability to adapt to changes and grow with the company.

Consideration:

In a start-up or new company, roles can evolve rapidly, so look for flexible individuals who are eager to learn and take on new challenges.

4. Work Ethic and Attitude:

Focus:

Seek candidates with a strong work ethic and a positive attitude.

Consideration:

Employees who are diligent, reliable, and have a can-do attitude are invaluable, especially in the early stages of a business.

5. Cost-to-Company (CTC):

Focus:

Consider the cost implications of hiring, including salary, benefits, and any other compensation.

Consideration:

Balance offering competitive packages with the financial realities of a new business.

6. Diversity and Inclusion:

Focus:

Aim for a diverse workforce.

Consideration:

Diversity in backgrounds, perspectives, and skills can foster innovation and a more dynamic workplace.

7. Legal Compliance:

Focus:

Ensure compliance with labour laws and regulations.

Consideration:

Understand and adhere to legal requirements related to hiring, including contracts, benefits, and workplace policies.

8. Future Scalability:

Focus:

Consider how the manpower will scale with the business's growth.

Consideration:

Look for candidates who can handle expanded roles as the company grows.

9. Team Dynamics:

Focus:

Think about how new hires will fit into and contribute to existing or future team dynamics.

Consideration:

Effective collaboration and team synergy are crucial for productivity and morale.

10. Background Checks:

Focus:

Conduct thorough background checks.

Consideration:

Verify candidate credentials, work history, and references to ensure reliability and integrity.

11. Training and Development Needs:

Focus:

Assess the training needs of new employees.

Consideration:

Determine if the candidate will require extensive training or if they can hit the ground running.

12. Succession Planning:

Focus:

Consider the potential for internal promotions and succession.

Consideration:

Hiring with an eye on future leadership can help ensure long-term stability.

Conclusion

The process of selecting manpower is critical for setting a new business on the path to success. It's about finding the right balance of skills, cultural fit, growth potential, and cost-effectiveness. A thoughtful approach to hiring can create a strong, dynamic team capable of driving the business forward.

"Fair pay for a fair day's work is the cornerstone of a thriving workplace."

Chapter 15

Fundraising and Salary Management for New Ventures

Financing Growth and Managing Compensation in New Ventures

Embarking on a new venture requires not only a compelling vision but also adequate financial resources to bring that vision to life. In this chapter, we explore the intricacies of fundraising and salary management for start-ups and emerging ventures. From bootstrapping and crowdfunding to venture capital and angel investment, we delve into various funding options available to entrepreneurs at different stages of their journey. Learn how to create a robust financial plan and allocate resources effectively to support business growth while ensuring competitive compensation for your team. Navigate the complexities of equity distribution and employee stock options, striking a balance between rewarding early contributors and preserving ownership stakes. Discover best practices for salary negotiation and structuring compensation packages to attract and retain top talent in a competitive market. Whether you're seeking investment opportunities or managing cash flow, this chapter provides valuable insights and strategies to fuel the success of your new venture.

Let us discuss on how newly formed organizations, companies, new entrepreneurs raise and manage funds to pay salary and compensation to their employees.

Raising and managing funds for salary and compensation in newly formed organizations, companies, or start-ups is a critical aspect of ensuring the stability and growth of the business.

Here's a comprehensive guide on how new entrepreneurs can approach this challenge:

1. Bootstrapping:

Explanation:

Bootstrapping involves self-funding the business using personal savings, revenue generated by the business, or minimal external financing.

Advantages:

Full control over the business.
Minimal debt and external obligations.
Forces efficient resource utilization.

Tips:

Prioritize essential expenses.
Reinvest profits into the business.
Look for cost-effective solutions.

2. Angel Investors:

Explanation:

Angel investors are individuals who provide financial support to start-ups in exchange for equity or convertible debt.

Advantages:

Expertise and mentorship often accompany the investment.
Allows for faster growth compared to bootstrapping.

Tips:

Create a compelling business plan.
Network to connect with potential angel investors.
Communicate the business's potential for growth and success.

3. Venture Capital:

Explanation:

Venture capitalists are professional groups that manage pooled funds from various investors, providing capital to start-ups in exchange for equity.

Advantages:

Significant capital injection.
Access to networks and resources.

Tips:

Be prepared for a thorough due diligence process.
Develop a scalable and high-growth business model.
Seek venture capital firms aligned with your industry.

4. Crowdfunding:

Explanation:

Crowdfunding involves raising small amounts of money from a large number of people, typically through online platforms.

Advantages:

Diverse funding sources.
Validates the business idea in the market.

Tips:

Create an engaging crowdfunding campaign.
Clearly communicate the value proposition.
Offer attractive rewards for backers.

5. Government Grants and Subsidies:

Explanation:

Many governments offer grants, subsidies, or low-interest loans to support start-ups in specific industries.

Advantages:

Non-dilutive funding.
Government support and validation.

Tips:

Research available grants and eligibility criteria.
Prepare a detailed proposal demonstrating alignment with grant objectives.

6. Business Loans:

Explanation:

Traditional business loans from banks or online lenders provide a lump sum amount that needs to be repaid with interest.

Advantages:

Structured repayment plans.
Allows for immediate capital infusion.

Tips:

Maintain a good credit score.
Develop a robust business plan to present to lenders.
Consider the interest rates and repayment terms.

7. Strategic Partnerships:

Explanation:

Collaborate with other businesses for mutual benefit, which may include financial support.

Advantages:

Shared resources and expertise.
Can lead to new business opportunities.

Tips:

Identify potential partners aligned with your goals.
Clearly define the terms and expectations of the partnership.

8. Employee Stock Ownership Plans (ESOPs):

Explanation:

ESOPs allow employees to own shares in the company, providing them with a stake in the business's success.

Advantages:

Attracts and retains top talent.
Aligns employee interests with company performance.

Tips:

Establish clear guidelines for the distribution of shares.
Communicate the benefits of ESOPs to employees.

9. Revenue-Based Financing:

Explanation:

Investors provide capital in exchange for a percentage of the company's revenue until a predefined return is achieved.

Advantages:

Tied to revenue, aligning interests.
No equity dilution until revenue is generated.

Tips:

Clearly define the terms of revenue sharing.
Ensure the business model supports regular revenue generation.

10. Strategic Pre-Sales:

Explanation:

Offer early access, discounts, or exclusive perks to customers in exchange for pre-payment.

Advantages:

Generates revenue before the product or service launch.
Validates market interest.

Tips:

Clearly communicate the value of pre-sale offers.
Set realistic delivery timelines.

Conclusion

Managing funds for salaries and compensation in a new organization requires a strategic and diversified approach. Entrepreneurs should carefully evaluate the options available based on their business model, growth plans, and industry dynamics. Combining multiple funding sources and maintaining financial discipline are key factors in ensuring the successful establishment and growth of a new venture.

"Invest in your employees, and they'll invest in your success."

Chapter 16

Managing Funds for New Ventures: Safeguarding Employees and Business

Financial Stewardship in New Ventures: Protecting Employees and Business Assets

As entrepreneurs navigate the dynamic landscape of new ventures, managing funds effectively becomes paramount to ensuring the sustainability and growth of both the business and its workforce. In this chapter, we explore the crucial role of financial stewardship in safeguarding employees and business assets. From establishing sound budgeting practices to implementing robust internal controls, we delve into strategies for prudent financial management that mitigate risks and foster resilience. Learn how to allocate resources strategically to support employee compensation while maintaining operational efficiency and liquidity. Explore innovative approaches to funding employee benefits and safeguarding against financial disruptions, such as insurance and contingency planning. Gain insights into the importance of transparency and accountability in financial decision-making, fostering trust and confidence among stakeholders. Whether you're bootstrapping a start-up or scaling a growing enterprise, this chapter equips you with the knowledge and tools to navigate financial challenges effectively and protect the interests of both your employees and your business.

In this chapter, we will explore how newly formed organizations, companies, and entrepreneurs manage their available funds or future earnings to protect their employees and ensure the overall stability of their businesses.

For newly formed organizations, start-ups, or entrepreneurs, managing available or newly acquired funds to safeguard both their employees and the overall business is a critical balancing act.

Here's a precise guide on how to approach this:

1. Budgeting and Financial Planning:

Strategy:

Create a detailed budget that includes all expenses, such as salaries, operational costs, and overheads.

Goal:

Ensure a clear understanding of financial inflows and outflows to avoid overspending and ensure sustainability.

2. Cash Flow Management:

Strategy:

Monitor cash flow regularly to ensure there's enough cash to cover critical expenses, including payroll.

Goal:

Prevent cash shortages that can jeopardize both employee compensation and business operations.

3. Cost Control:

Strategy:

Identify and cut unnecessary expenses. Opt for cost-effective solutions without compromising quality.

Goal:

Free up resources to prioritize employee compensation and critical business investments.

4. Emergency Fund:

Strategy:

Set aside a portion of funds as a reserve for unexpected expenses.

Goal:

Provide a financial cushion to protect the business and employees during tough times.

5. Diversifying Revenue Streams:

Strategy:

Explore multiple revenue channels to reduce dependency on a single source.

Goal:

Enhance financial stability, providing more security for business operations and employee salaries.

6. Prudent Hiring Practices:

Strategy:

Hire essential personnel initially and consider contract or freelance workers for non-core functions.

Goal:

Keep the payroll manageable while the business is still growing.

7. Investing in Employees:

Strategy:

Offer non-monetary benefits like flexible working hours, a positive work environment, and growth opportunities.

Goal:

Enhance employee satisfaction and retention, which can be more cost-effective than high salaries in the early stages.

8. Transparent Communication:

Strategy:

Maintain open communication lines with employees regarding the company's financial health and compensation policies.

Goal:

Build trust and understanding, ensuring employees feel valued and part of the journey.

9. Regular Financial Reviews:

Strategy:

Conduct frequent financial reviews to assess the health of the business and adjust plans as necessary.

Goal:

Stay agile and responsive to changing financial circumstances.

10. Legal Compliance and Risk Management:

Strategy:

Ensure compliance with tax laws, labour laws, and other regulations to avoid legal penalties and risks.

Goal:

Protect the business from legal risks and financial losses.

Conclusion

Managing funds effectively in a new business involves a combination of careful financial planning, cost control, revenue diversification, and employee-focused strategies. By balancing these elements, entrepreneurs can safeguard their businesses and ensure that they are positioned both to support their employees and to grow sustainably.

"Compensation is not just about the money; it's about acknowledging hard work and dedication."

Chapter 17

Exploring Salary Systems Across Global Economies

In an increasingly interconnected world, understanding the nuances of salary systems across different economies is essential for businesses and professionals alike. In this chapter, we embark on a comparative exploration of salary structures and practices, examining key differences and similarities across diverse economic landscapes. From examining the impact of cultural norms and regulatory frameworks on compensation practices to analyzing trends in wage growth and income inequality, we delve into the complexities of salary systems on a global scale. Gain insights into the factors shaping salary disparities and the implications for talent attraction, retention, and mobility. Explore case studies highlighting successful strategies for aligning compensation with organizational objectives in various economic contexts. Whether you're expanding into new markets or seeking to optimize your compensation strategy domestically, this chapter provides valuable perspectives and actionable insights to inform your decision-making and drive sustainable growth.

This chapter is related to the salary systems in under-developed, developing and developed countries, their key features, advantages and disadvantages in general.

Salary systems vary across under-developed, developing, and developed countries due to differences in economic conditions, labour markets, and regulatory environments.

Salary systems in various developed, underdeveloped and developing countries - Their pros and cons or their advantages and disadvantages

The salary systems in various developed, underdeveloped, and developing countries have their own unique set of advantages and disadvantages depending on the level of development and economic stability.

These systems play a crucial role in determining the compensation employees receive for their work. Understanding the advantages and disadvantages of different salary systems is crucial to analysing the effectiveness and fairness of compensation structures across different economies and can shed light on the complexities involved in ensuring fair and equitable pay.

In developed countries, such as those in Europe or North America, salary systems are often based on factors such as education, experience, and job performance. This merit-based approach aims to reward employees for their skills and contributions to the organization. One advantage of this system is that it motivates individuals to continuously improve their skills and excel in their roles.

In developed countries, the salary systems are often more structured and regulated, offering higher wages and better benefits to employees. This can lead to a higher standard of living and increased job satisfaction. One advantage of a well-structured salary system is that it promotes fairness and equity among employees. It ensures that individuals are compensated based on their skills, experience, and contribution to the organization. This can motivate employees to perform better and increase productivity within the workforce.

In developed countries, the salary systems are often characterized by higher wages and comprehensive benefits packages. This allows employees to enjoy a higher standard of living and access to better healthcare, education, and social security. Additionally, these systems typically prioritize merit-based pay raises and performance evaluations, rewarding employees for their skills and contributions.

However, one disadvantage of merit-based salary systems is that they can perpetuate inequalities if certain groups have historically been disadvantaged or discriminated against.

For example, women or minority groups may face barriers to accessing higher-paying positions or may be paid less than their counterparts with similar qualifications.

One another potential disadvantage of salary systems in developed countries is the high cost of living that accompanies higher wages. This can lead to increased competition for jobs and a higher cost burden on employers. Additionally, there may be a greater emphasis on individual performance metrics rather than holistic team or organizational success.

In underdeveloped and developing countries, salary systems may be influenced by factors such as local economic conditions, government regulations, or cultural norms. In some cases, there may be a lack of transparency or standardized practices when it comes to determining salaries. This can lead to disparities and unfair treatment among employees.

One advantage of these salary systems is that they often prioritize providing a basic living wage for employees who may otherwise struggle to meet their basic needs. In some cases, government-mandated minimum wage laws aim to protect workers from exploitation. These salary systems may be more focused on providing basic sustenance rather than offering competitive wages.

While lower labour costs can attract foreign investment in these economies, it can also perpetuate income inequality within society.

Moreover, without adequate compensation structures in place, it becomes difficult for individuals to break free from cycles of poverty or improve their overall quality of life.

A disadvantage of these systems is that they may not adequately reward individuals for their skills or incentivize high performance. This can hinder productivity and limit opportunities for professional growth.

In underdeveloped or developing countries, the salary systems may face challenges such as low minimum wage standards, limited access to essential benefits such as healthcare or retirement plans, and a lack of job security.

They are less regulated and offer lower wages. This can result in a lower standard of living for employees.

Overall, it is important to recognize that there is no one-size-fits-all approach when it comes to salary systems across different countries. Each system has its unique advantages and disadvantages based on the specific socio-economic context in which it operates. Striving for fairness and equity in compensation remains a constant challenge that requires ongoing evaluation and improvement.

Another disadvantage of some salary systems is that they may perpetuate income inequality. In some cases, certain industries or professions may offer significantly higher salaries compared to others, leading to disparities in wealth distribution. This can create social unrest and dissatisfaction among those who feel unfairly compensated for their work.

It is important for governments and organizations to carefully consider the pros and cons of different salary systems while taking into account factors such as cost of living, economic conditions, and societal expectations.

Striking a balance between fair compensation for employees while promoting economic growth is crucial for sustainable development in any country.

Here's an overview of the key features, advantages, and disadvantages of salary systems in each category:

Under-Developed Countries:

Key Features:

Low Base Salaries:

Typically, base salaries are lower due to lower overall economic development.

Limited Benefits:

Comprehensive employee benefits may be scarce.

Informal Labor Markets:

Many jobs may be in the informal sector with limited job security.

Advantages:

Lower Labor Costs:

Businesses may benefit from lower labour costs.

Flexibility:

Informal structures can provide flexibility in employment arrangements.

Disadvantages:

Poverty Cycle:

Low salaries contribute to the poverty cycle.

Limited Professional Development:

Limited resources for training and development.

Developing Countries:

Key Features:

Economic Growth:

Generally, experiencing economic growth with a growing workforce.

Diverse Workforce:

A mix of formal and informal employment sectors.

Emerging Benefits:

Benefits may be expanding but still less comprehensive than in developed nations.

Advantages:

Cost-Effective Talent:

Skilled labour may be available at a lower cost.

Growth Opportunities:

Opportunities for professional and economic growth.

Disadvantages:

Inequality:

Disparities between high and low-skilled jobs may contribute to inequality.

Regulatory Challenges:

Regulatory frameworks may be less robust.

Developed Countries:

Key Features:

Higher Base Salaries:

Generally, higher base salaries are due to economic prosperity.

Comprehensive Benefits:

Extensive employee benefits packages, including health insurance, retirement plans, etc.

Formal Employment:

High proportion of formal employment contracts.

Advantages:

High Quality of Life:

Higher salaries contribute to a higher quality of life.

Skilled Workforce:

Access to a highly skilled and educated workforce.

Disadvantages:

High Labor Costs:

Businesses may face higher labour costs.

Rigid Labor Markets:

Formal structures can sometimes be less flexible.

General Considerations:

1. Globalization:

Advantages:

Globalization allows for the exchange of talent, skills, and expertise.

Disadvantages:

Can contribute to wage disparities between developed and developing nations.

2. Regulatory Environment:

Advantages:

Robust regulatory frameworks in developed countries protect workers' rights.

Disadvantages:

Strict regulations can be burdensome for businesses.

3. Talent Mobility:

Advantages:

Skilled workers in developed countries can find opportunities globally.

Disadvantages:

Brain drain can be a challenge for underdeveloped nations.

4. Technology Impact:

Advantages:

Developed nations often lead in adopting and benefiting from technology.

Disadvantages:

Job displacement can occur due to automation.

Salary systems reflect the economic development, labour market dynamics, and regulatory environments of countries. While under-developed nations may face challenges with lower salaries and informal structures, they may offer flexibility. Developing nations experience growth with a mix of formal and informal employment. Developed countries feature higher base salaries, comprehensive benefits, and formalized employment structures, contributing to a higher quality of life for employees. Globalization, regulatory environments, talent mobility, and technological advancements further shape salary systems globally.

Conclusion

In conclusion, the pros and cons of salary systems vary across different countries based on their economic development levels. Policymakers need to strike a balance between fair compensation practices that provide employees with a decent quality of life while also fostering economic growth and sustainability within their respective nations.

"Investing in fair compensation is investing in the foundation of a strong and sustainable business."

Chapter 18

Thinking Out of the Box

Embracing Innovative Approaches to Compensation

Welcome to a chapter that challenges conventional wisdom and encourages creative thinking in the realm of compensation. In "Thinking Out of the Box," we explore innovative strategies and unconventional practices that redefine traditional notions of pay and reward. From exploring alternative forms of compensation beyond monetary incentives to leveraging technology and data analytics to personalize employee rewards, we delve into cutting-edge approaches that inspire engagement and drive performance. Discover how forward-thinking organizations are experimenting with flexible work arrangements, gamification, and peer-to-peer recognition to foster a culture of appreciation and empowerment. Through insightful case studies and thought-provoking examples, we invite you to push the boundaries of conventional compensation practices and embrace bold ideas that resonate with the modern workforce. Join us on a journey of discovery as we explore the limitless possibilities of compensation innovation and chart a course towards a more dynamic and rewarding future.

Now have a look at this example. This example presents an interesting perspective on business sectors and compensation models:

There are three main types of business sectors: production, service, and trading. Within the service sector, there are two sub–categories - paid service and absolute service. Paid services, such as telecommunications, directly charge their customers. Absolute services, such as those provided by teachers in pre-primary and primary schools, police officers, army personnel, government health professionals, and other civil service providers, typically do not directly generate significant income, except for some applicable charges.

My viewpoint is that salaries should be reserved only for absolute service providers. For other business categories, employees should receive a share of the net profits. This share can be allocated in various forms, such as allowances, provident funds, life insurance, health/ medical insurance, etc. However, compensation must be a percentage of the profit and not a fixed salary amount. Fixed salaries merely keep employees afloat without supporting their overall growth. This is a primary reason why underdeveloped and developing countries struggle to progress. These nations haven't crafted a financial system that truly benefits their citizens.

We need to consider national economic systems and their impact on the financial conditions of citizens. The overall and general salary system often fails to effectively change the financial conditions of citizens. A nation's economy should be cycled; if the national wealth does not circulate or revolve throughout the nation, it fails to reach every citizen. The polarization of national wealth is always dangerous for that nation. In such scenarios, people tend to try to take money from those who have it in surplus. Cheating, fraud, scams, robberies, dacoity, systems like "HAWALA", and income tax evasion are well-known consequences of the current economic system. Therefore, underdeveloped and developing countries should adopt a cycled economic theory by studying a cyclical economic theory carefully, instead of the trickle-down economic theory.

Cyclical economic theory refers to the analysis and understanding of economic fluctuations that occur in a cyclical pattern over time. These fluctuations are often characterized by periods of expansion (economic booms) followed by contractions (economic recessions or downturns). The cyclical economic theory suggests that economies go through recurring phases of growth and decline, and these cycles are a normal part of the economic system.

Key components of cyclical economic theory include:

1. Boom (Expansion):

During this phase, the economy experiences robust growth. There is an increase in economic activity, employment, and consumer spending. Businesses expand, and investments are high.

2. Bust (Contraction or Recession):

This phase involves a slowdown in economic activity. Employment may decline, consumer spending may decrease, and businesses may cut back on investments. A recession is characterized by a decrease in the overall economic output.

3. Trough:

The trough is the bottom point of the economic cycle, where economic activity is at its lowest. It marks the end of the recession and the beginning of the recovery.

4. Recovery:

During the recovery phase, the economy starts to bounce back from the trough. Economic activity begins to pick up, employment increases, and consumer confidence improves.

This cyclical pattern is often referred to as the business cycle. Various factors contribute to these cycles, including changes in consumer spending, business investments, government policies, and external shocks. Economists and policymakers study these cycles to understand the drivers and to formulate strategies to manage and mitigate the impact of economic downturns. Monetary and fiscal policies are often employed to stabilize the economy during different phases of the business cycle.

Using the term "cycled economic theory" instead of "cyclical economic theory" would represent a departure from established economic terminology and might lead to confusion. "Cyclical economic theory" is a well-understood concept in economics, referring to the natural and recurring phases of expansion and contraction in an economy.

However, if we propose a new or specific economic theory, we certainly have the freedom to coin a new term.

"Cycled economic theory" is meant to describe an economic system where national money/wealth circulates through small, interconnected cycles to ensure broader economic stability and equitable distribution.

Let's consider the example of the Nitrogen Cycle. The Nitrogen Cycle is a natural process that helps maintain a constant level of atmospheric nitrogen. However, this large cycle comprises many smaller cycles and life cycles of its various components, such as lightning during the monsoon, nitrogen-fixing bacteria, nitrifying bacteria, denitrifying bacteria, plants, animals, industrial and factory emissions, and marine activities. The Nitrogen Cycle is a crucial process that involves the transformation of nitrogen into different forms within the environment.

Here's a brief overview of the Nitrogen Cycle, including its key components, for a better understanding of what 'cycled' means.

1. Nitrogen Fixation:

Nitrogen gas (N_2) from the atmosphere through lightning is converted into ammonia (NH_3) or ammonium ions (NH_4^+) by nitrogen-fixing bacteria in the soil.

2. Nitrification:

Ammonia or ammonium is converted into nitrite (NO_2^-) and then into nitrate (NO_3^-) by nitrifying bacteria. This process makes nitrogen in the soil available for plant uptake.

3. Assimilation:

Plants absorb nitrate ions from the soil and incorporate nitrogen into their organic molecules, such as proteins and nucleic acids.

4. Ammonification:

Decomposers break down organic matter (dead plants and animals) into ammonia or ammonium ions. This releases nitrogen back into the soil.

5. Denitrification:

Denitrifying bacteria convert nitrate in the soil back into nitrogen gas, releasing it into the atmosphere. This completes the cycle.

Throughout the nitrogen cycle, nitrogen transitions between the atmosphere, soil, and living organisms in various forms, such as nitrogen gas, ammonia, ammonium ions, nitrite, and nitrate. This cycle is essential for maintaining the availability of nitrogen, a critical element for the formation of proteins and nucleic acids, in ecosystems. The balance between these processes ensures that nitrogen is continually recycled and available for use by plants and other organisms. Importantly, each element of the cycle - namely, the organisms engaged in nitrogen fixation, nitrification, assimilation, ammonification, and denitrification operates within its life cycle, yet collectively contributes to the larger nitrogen cycle.

To draw an analogy with natural cycles, such as the nitrogen cycle, we could elaborate on how the smaller economic cycles interact and contribute to the overall stability and health of the national economy. This could involve detailing mechanisms for wealth redistribution and re-utilization, small-scale economic interactions, and how they collectively contribute to larger economic goals. If we start thinking about this seriously, we shall overcome challenges one day, undoubtedly. What we have to do is we have to think about this very seriously and consciously.

Remember, the key to introducing a new term or concept is clarity and precision in its definition and explanation. People need to understand how the proposed "cycled economic theory" differs from traditional concepts and how it operates within the context of national and global economies.

The concept of integrating various human capacities and resources into a common economic cycle is intriguing and aligns with some holistic economic theories. The eight elements i.e. the eight powers of the human world viz. – time, experience, knowledge, skill, ideas or concepts, labour, contacts, and money – are indeed vital components of a productive economy.

Let's briefly explore how this concept aligns with economic principles:

1. Time:

This is a fundamental resource in economics. Efficient time management can enhance productivity and economic output. The population of any country that has a lot of leisure time is its most powerful resource. This population can be easily or forcibly engaged in either destructive or constructive work. That country should engage this manpower in constructive activities. However, this can sometimes hamper the political agendas of that country, as such a population can be an easy target to provoke over trivial issues that help the political parties during elections.

2. Experience:

Experienced individuals contribute to the economy by improving processes, mentoring others, and making informed decisions.

3. Knowledge:

The foundation of innovation and progress, knowledge drives economic growth through technological advancements and improved methodologies.

4. Skill:

Skilled labour is crucial for a diverse and robust economy. A skilled workforce can lead to higher productivity and economic growth.

5. Ideas or Concepts:

Innovation drives economic development. New ideas and concepts can lead to new products, services, and ways of doing business.

6. Labour:

The workforce is the backbone of any economy. Labour, both skilled and unskilled, performs the essential tasks that keep the economy running. The concept of labour consists of both physical and mental labour. If this national resource is used with more dignity and better compensation, the national economy will be improved.

7. Contacts:

Networks and relationships can open markets, facilitate trade, and foster collaborations that benefit the economy.

8. Money/ Wealth

Serving as a medium of exchange, a store of value, and a unit of account, money is essential for facilitating economic transactions. In the new concept of a cycled economy, this last but crucial component of the human world can act as a thread weaving the above seven components together to create a beautiful garland, i.e., a complete, ever-living national economy. Nature teaches us that anything that completes its cycle never dies, while that which cannot complete its cycle ultimately vanishes. If we want to keep our economy alive forever, we must ensure it completes its cycle.

By integrating these elements into a cohesive economic model, we envision an economy that values and utilizes all forms of human capital and resources. This approach could lead to a more balanced and inclusive economic system where each element supports and enhances the others, contributing to overall national wealth and potentially ensuring a more equitable distribution of resources.

However, the challenge lies in the practical implementation of such a model. Balancing these elements without bias and effectively integrating them into a functioning economic system would require careful planning, policy formulation, and possibly a shift in societal and economic paradigms. The idea, while conceptually sound and inclusive, would need a detailed framework and strategy for practical application.

In a cycled economic model, income tax slabs would be optimized to ensure money keeps rotating throughout the nation. This approach would foster financial equality and lead to the evolution of the nation's GDP at a point of balanced equilibrium. If income were directly proportional to the efforts and revenue generated for a company or nation, it could significantly alter the poverty landscape. However, there's a fear that such a system would challenge the availability of cheap manpower and affect political agendas.

A detailed discussion about the cycled economy will be presented in my upcoming book, as the focus of this current book is solely on salary and compensation. Let's adhere to this topic within the scope of the current book.

Now coming to the point of fair salary and compensation - Let's consider a small cloth/ garment shop as an example. Assume I start one with two employees, one for the gents' section and another for the ladies' section, making us a team of three. I take a bank loan, with associated Equated Monthly Instalments. There are additional expenses like rent, utility bills, local government taxes, income tax, GST, transport and communication charges, and some miscellaneous costs. I also set aside funds for next month's inventory purchases, insurance for the business and employees, and a buffer for unforeseen circumstances. If our gross income each month exceeds our total expenses, here's what I propose:

Calculate the net income by deducting expenses from gross income. Then, divide the net income into four parts, two for me as the owner and one for each employee. Why divide the share into two parts for the owner? Because not only the owner, but also their family, is either passively or actively involved in building up the business. The other part of the share is for them. It is the owner and their family who are going to suffer or benefit from the business. The owner's family has invested their time, money, support, dreams, and has taken risks for the business. This is not the case with employees.

For instance, if our net income in a month is 1 lakh, I would take 50k, and each employee would receive 25k. In this system, employees are motivated to work harder and contribute more, as their income is directly proportional to their efforts and not a fixed amount. This approach could foster positive societal changes and help alleviate poverty, especially in small businesses. While it might be challenging in large businesses, it is certainly feasible in smaller ones.

In essence, offering a share of net profits instead of a fixed salary can instigate positive changes in the financial system. By not adopting this approach, I would merely be sustaining my employees at a basic level, solely for the benefit of my business. This approach is counterproductive to humanity. If we can financially empower our employees, why choose not to? The selfishness of business owners and the unawareness of employees about their rights and capabilities are significant contributors to employee poverty. Setting aside selfish motives and embracing a more humanitarian approach can lead to sustainable societal changes.

Insights into managing personal finances and fostering employee engagement:

Not only that, but I also need to consider their routine expenses from their income. I would suggest the ratio of 40:60, i.e., 40% for direct expenses and 60% for savings, investments, and personal growth. They should spend only - 40% of their income from the shop, i.e. from 25k, on routine household expenses like grocery, utility bills, etc. 20% of the 25k should be saved, and some part of it should be used for investments, 20% should be reserved for children's health and education, additional insurances that are not covered by the shop as part of their employment benefits, and adult health issues, 10% should be allocated for social involvement such as relatives' or friends' birthdays, marriages, festivals, etc., and the remaining 10% should be invested in their personal growth through new ideas to improve and elevate their standard of living.

These percentage distributions are flexible and can be adjusted, except for the savings and investment component. Their personal and family insurance is covered by the shop as part of their employment benefits. Savings, along with life and health insurance, are crucial elements of any salary and compensation package for employees. If a salary package fails to address these aspects, it can be considered exploitation and should be avoided. In underdeveloped and developing countries, some individuals in the production and service sectors challenge the national laws made for employees and often disobey them. This issue must be taken very seriously and should be met with appropriate punishment. However, this generally occurs due to the illiteracy of labourers and or their helplessness.

If someone claims to have generated or created employment for 100 people but fails to provide them with appropriate and satisfactory salary and compensation, then they are, in fact, the biggest hypocrites. Instead of creating genuine employment opportunities, they are exploiting cheap labor for their own benefit. By profiting from the sweat and toil of workers, they are enriching themselves while their employees remain economically stagnant. This creates a significant disparity in their financial status. Unfortunately, such individuals often receive undue attention and respect from society, with many considering them to be great philanthropists. However, in reality, they are exploiting those 100 people. It is imperative that we identify such hypocrites within our society and demand fair wages, compensation, and a share in the net profits for the workers.

Poverty doesn't dictate how much we earn; instead, it dictates how we manage what we have earned. It is not determined by how much we earn, but by how we use what we earn. Poverty may be a temporary state of life if we learn to manage what we earn judicially.

Before being appointed as labourers/employees, they should be informed about their rights and benefits, along with their duties and the expected discipline.

Conclusion

When employees feel as though the business is their own, they work with dedication and contribute to its profitability. Allowing them to engage in discussions with the company's policymakers ensures they are not just at the receiving end of decisions. I like to discuss with my employees about new trends in clothing shops, customer preferences, fashion trends, availability of materials at factory or wholesale prices, etc. This way, I can create a real business environment in my shop.

"A transparent and equitable compensation structure fosters trust and loyalty among employees."

Chapter 19

Financial Equality Within Non-Government Organizations

In this chapter, we embark on a crucial exploration of financial equality within non-governmental organizations (NGOs). As we delve into "Financial Equality Within Non-Government Organizations," we confront the disparities that often exist in compensation structures and address strategies for fostering greater equity. From examining the impact of wage gaps on organizational culture to advocating for transparent salary policies, we delve into actionable steps that NGOs can take to promote fairness and inclusivity.

Maintaining financial equality among NGO employees involves ensuring fair and equitable compensation, benefits, and opportunities for professional growth.

Here are some strategies to achieve this:

1. Fair Compensation:

Establish transparent salary structures based on job roles, responsibilities, and experience levels. Regularly review and adjust salaries to ensure they are competitive and equitable within the industry and region.

Example:

An NGO establishes salary bands for different job roles based on industry standards and local cost of living. For instance, a project manager in a high-cost city might receive a higher salary compared to a project manager in a rural area. Regular salary reviews are conducted to ensure that salaries remain competitive and equitable.

2. Equal Access to Benefits:

Provide equal access to benefits such as health insurance, retirement plans, paid time off, and professional development opportunities for all employees, regardless of their position or tenure.

Example:

All employees of an NGO, regardless of their position, are eligible for the same health insurance plan with coverage for medical, dental, and vision care. Similarly, all employees have access to the same retirement savings plan with matching contributions from the organization.

3. Performance-Based Rewards:

Implement performance-based reward systems that recognize and reward employees based on their contributions, achievements, and impact within the organization. This helps to ensure that compensation and rewards are linked to merit rather than bias or favouritism.

Example:

At the end of each year, employees participate in performance evaluations where they are assessed based on their achievements, contributions to the organization's mission, and demonstration of core values. Those who exceed expectations receive bonuses or merit-based salary increases.

4. Promotion and Advancement Opportunities:

Create pathways for career advancement and promotion based on merit, skills, and qualifications rather than personal connections or biases. Offer training, mentoring, and leadership development programs to support employees' professional growth and advancement within the organization.

Example:

An NGO offers professional development opportunities such as leadership training workshops, skill-building courses, and mentorship programs to all employees. When positions become available for advancement, internal candidates are encouraged to apply, and promotions are based on qualifications and performance.

5. Transparency and Accountability:

Maintain transparency in decision-making processes related to compensation, promotions, and benefits. Communicate the criteria and rationale behind these decisions to employees to foster trust and accountability within the organization.

Example:

During annual performance reviews, managers provide detailed feedback to employees on their performance and discuss potential areas for improvement. The organization also publishes an annual report that outlines its compensation philosophy, including how salaries are determined and any changes made to benefits.

6. Diversity, Equity, and Inclusion (DEI) Initiatives:

Implement DEI initiatives aimed at addressing systemic barriers and promoting a culture of inclusion and belonging within the organization. This may include unconscious bias training, diversity recruitment strategies, and creating safe spaces for open dialogue and feedback.

Example:

The NGO implements diversity recruitment strategies to ensure that job postings reach a diverse pool of candidates. They also conduct regular DEI training sessions for employees and establish employee resource groups to provide support and foster a sense of belonging among underrepresented groups.

7. Regular Evaluation and Feedback:

Conduct regular evaluations and feedback sessions to assess employees' satisfaction with their compensation, benefits, and opportunities for advancement. Use this feedback to identify areas for improvement and make necessary adjustments to maintain financial equality within the organization.

Example:

The organization conducts quarterly employee engagement surveys to gather feedback on various aspects of the workplace, including compensation and benefits. HR regularly meets with employees to discuss their career goals and aspirations and address any concerns they may have regarding their compensation or opportunities for advancement.

By implementing these strategies, NGOs can ensure that their employees are treated fairly, compensated equitably, and provided with opportunities for professional growth and advancement, ultimately contributing to a more inclusive and sustainable organizational culture. NGOs can create a workplace culture that values fairness, transparency, and inclusivity, thereby maintaining financial equality among their employees.

If we want to bring financial equality within NGOs, the basic salary should be the same for all, whether they are the CEO, MD, director, manager, gatekeeper, watchman, housekeeping staff, or permanent farm labourer. There should not be a difference in their basic salary. Additionally, commonly applicable allowances such as travel allowance, dearness allowance, medical/ health insurance and life insurance covering their families, gratuity, and provident funds should be the same.

In addition, providing certain extra allowances is necessary to properly reflect the roles, positions, talents, responsibilities, and seniority of employees. These additional allowances may lead to slight variations in the overall salary packages.

The 'PARSIST' system of compensation is a framework that NGOs can apply to their employees.

This system offers a comprehensive package that addresses various aspects of compensation for NGO volunteers. Let's delve into each allowance, along with examples, features, and necessities.

1. Promotion Allowance (P):

Definition:

Promotion allowance is provided to volunteers who demonstrate exceptional performance and are promoted to higher positions or roles within the organization. This process doesn't require a specific period. Anyone with the capability of being promoted can achieve this milestone.

Example:

For instance, a volunteer coordinator who consistently exceeds expectations and demonstrates leadership qualities may be promoted to a managerial position, accompanied by a promotion allowance.

Features:

It rewards advancement and encourages career growth within the organization.

Necessity:

This allowance recognizes and motivates volunteers to strive for excellence, contributing to organizational success.

2. Achievement Allowance (A):

Definition:

Achievement allowance, also called a performance allowance, is granted to volunteers who accomplish specific goals or milestones that contribute significantly to the organization's mission.

Example:

For example, a fundraising volunteer who successfully raises a substantial amount of funds for a specific project may receive an achievement allowance as recognition for their accomplishment.

Features:

It recognizes and incentivizes exceptional performance and goal attainment.

Necessity:

This allowance motivates volunteers to set and achieve ambitious objectives, fostering a culture of excellence and accountability.

3. Responsibility Allowance (R):

Definition:

Responsibility allowance is provided to volunteers who take on additional duties, roles, or responsibilities beyond their regular scope of work. When volunteers recruited for a specific position in the organization carry out and fulfil their responsibilities with maximum precision and accuracy, they also become eligible for this allowance. This responsibility allowance can be converted into a position allowance in the case of schools, colleges, hospitals, organizational positions, etc. The percentage should vary according to the extent of responsibility they hold.

Example:

The principal of a school should have this allowance as it is the most responsible position within the school. Another example is - that a volunteer who takes on the responsibility of mentoring recruits or managing a critical project may receive a responsibility allowance after successfully completing it.

Features:

It compensates volunteers for the added workload and leadership responsibilities they undertake.

Necessity:

This allowance encourages volunteers to take on leadership roles and contribute to the organization's growth and development.

4. Seasonal Allowance for Workers (S):

Definition:

Seasonal allowance is granted to volunteers who work in roles or projects that require additional effort or commitment during specific seasons or periods.

Example:

For example, volunteers engaged in disaster relief efforts during hurricane season may receive a seasonal allowance to compensate for their increased availability and dedication. Farm workers require raincoats during the rainy season and warm clothes during winter. They also need extra remedies to protect themselves from the summer heat. Therefore, this allowance enables them to purchase the necessary materials.

Features:

It provides financial support to volunteers working on demanding or time-sensitive projects.

Necessity:

This allowance recognizes and rewards volunteers for their flexibility and dedication during critical periods. Furthermore, it fosters a sense of belonging among volunteers by covering their essential needs without impacting their remuneration.

5. Intellectual Allowance (I):

Definition:

Intellectual allowance is provided to volunteers who contribute valuable ideas, innovations, or intellectual property that enhance the organization's effectiveness or efficiency.

Example:

For instance, a volunteer who develops a new programmatic approach or technology solution to streamline operations may receive an intellectual allowance. This allowance is available to any volunteer or employee of the organization, regardless of their role or position.

Features:

It recognizes and incentivizes creativity, innovation, and intellectual contributions.

Necessity:

This allowance encourages volunteers to think critically, innovate, and contribute new ideas to address organizational challenges. Furthermore, it provides equal opportunity for everyone to contribute to the organization's improvement efforts. Whether an employee works as a gatekeeper, peon, or CEO, they can receive this allowance equally for their ideas or concepts that benefit the organization's growth.

6. Seniority Allowance (S):

Definition:

Seniority allowance is granted to volunteers based on their length of service or tenure with the organization.

Example:

Volunteers who have been with the organization for a certain number of years may receive a seniority allowance as a token of appreciation for their loyalty and dedication.

Features:

Rewards long-term commitment and loyalty to the organization.

Necessity:

Recognizes the contributions of seasoned volunteers and fosters retention and continuity within the organization.

7. Training Allowance (T):

Definition:

The training allowance is provided to volunteers to support their professional development, skills enhancement, and participation in training programs or workshops.

Example:

For instance, volunteers attending a specialized training session on project management may receive a training allowance to cover their expenses.

Features:

This allowance supports volunteers' continuous learning and skill development.

Necessity:

It invests in volunteers' growth and capacity building, enhancing their effectiveness and performance within the organization. Additionally, this allowance encourages volunteers and employees to undergo periodic training, helping them stay updated and potentially leading to the generation of new ideas. When an employee requests a particular training and successfully convinces the board of directors of its necessity and their interest in it, they are allowed to enrol, and the training allowance is provided.

By incorporating the PARSIST system of compensation, NGOs can provide a well-rounded and motivating compensation package that acknowledges and rewards volunteers for their contributions, achievements, and commitment, thereby fostering a culture of engagement, excellence, and continuous improvement within the organization.

As an employer, we have to drive the business, while as employees, we have to propel the business forward. This mutual effort, driving and propelling in the same direction with the same motivation, leads to successful business operations. Avoid making employees feel like servants or dependents; instead, foster a sense of belonging by treating them as valued members of the team. Encourage them to channel their passion for the business and empower them to soar with the support of the compensation you provide.

NGOs can introduce additional allowances as they feel necessary to incorporate into their organization based on their needs.

Suppose an NGO is running projects as a source of income. The manpower engaged in these projects should receive equal benefits in terms of salary and compensation packages. In fact, rather than offering them a fixed salary, consider providing them with a share in the permissible profit generated by these projects. Here, 'permissible' refers to the fact that although NGOs are generally non-profit organizations, they can engage in income-generating projects and allocate a portion of the profits to their manpower. The remaining profit generated by these projects has to be utilized for social work and services. The portion of the profit they can allocate for their manpower is known as the permissible profit share.

For example, if the basic amount to be paid to the manpower is 15k, and the calculated profit share is 20k, then they should receive 20k. However, if the calculated profit share falls below the basic amount, it is preferable to provide the basic amount. For instance, if the calculated profit share is 10k, the individual should still receive 15k to ensure they earn at least the basic income. In the following month, if the calculated profit share is 20k, then the excess amount from the previous month i.e. 5k, should be deducted, and 15k should be given.

This method ensures that no one earns below the basic income, while also providing an incentive for individuals to contribute to the success of the projects. In this way, we can maintain financial equality in our organization.

Conclusion

In conclusion, achieving financial equality within non-government organizations (NGOs) is paramount for fostering a fair and inclusive work environment. By implementing various strategies, including fair compensation, equal access to benefits, performance-based rewards, promotion opportunities, transparency, and diversity initiatives, NGOs can ensure that all employees are treated equitably and provided with opportunities for growth and advancement.

Additionally, adopting the PARSIST system of compensation can further enhance the compensation package for NGO volunteers, ensuring that their contributions are recognized and rewarded appropriately. This system provides a comprehensive framework that addresses various aspects of compensation, including promotion allowances, achievement allowances, responsibility allowances, seasonal allowances, intellectual allowances, seniority allowances, and training allowances.

Moreover, by distributing a share of the permissible profit generated by income-generating projects among the manpower, NGOs can provide an additional incentive for employees to contribute to the organization's success. This approach ensures that employees receive fair compensation while also aligning their interests with the organization's goals.

Ultimately, by prioritizing financial equality and implementing effective compensation and reward systems, NGOs can create a workplace culture that values fairness, transparency, and inclusivity, thereby fostering a motivated and engaged workforce dedicated to advancing the organization's mission and objectives.

"A well-designed compensation package is an investment in employee well-being and organizational success."

Chapter 20

Income Tax Histories: Global Perspectives

Exploring Income Tax Histories Globally

Welcome to a panoramic journey through the intricate landscapes of income tax histories across the globe. In "Income Tax Histories: Global Perspectives," we traverse continents and epochs to unravel the evolution of taxation systems and their profound impacts on societies. From the inception of income tax regimes to their contemporary manifestations, we dissect pivotal moments and trends that have shaped fiscal policies worldwide. Through compelling narratives and comparative analyses, we illuminate the diverse approaches to taxation embraced by nations spanning the globe. Join us as we uncover the socio-economic implications, political dynamics, and historical contexts that have defined income tax systems and continue to shape our economic landscapes.

Income tax history of some underdeveloped, developing and developed countries with their names and periodical changes related to the salary and compensation

A history of income tax in several underdeveloped, developing and developed countries, along with specific periodical changes related to salary and compensation, is quite extensive. However, here is a summarized overview of a few countries to illustrate how income tax systems have evolved. Please note that "underdeveloped" is a term that can be subjective and may not accurately represent the current state of these countries. It's often more appropriate to use "developing countries."

1. Nigeria

Pre-Independence:

Before independence in 1960, Nigeria had various forms of direct and indirect taxes influenced by British rule.

Post-Independence:

After independence, Nigeria reformed its tax system to better suit its economy.

The Personal Income Tax Act and Companies Income Tax Act were introduced.

Recent Changes:

Nigeria has been reforming its tax system to increase revenue and reduce dependence on oil.

Changes include adjustments in personal income tax slabs and the introduction of technology in tax collection.

2. Bangladesh

1971-1990s:

Following independence in 1971, Bangladesh inherited the tax structure from Pakistan. Initial reforms were slow.

2000s Onwards:

There's been a gradual modernization of the tax system, with a focus on widening the tax net and incorporating digital methods for tax collection.

Recent Trends:

Recent changes include adjustments in tax slabs for individual income and incentives for digital compliance.

3. Kenya

Pre-Independence:

Under British rule, the tax system was regressive and focused on revenue generation for the colonial administration.

Post-Independence:

Kenya restructured its tax system to promote economic growth and equity. This included the introduction of more progressive income tax rates.

21st Century:

Recent reforms focus on expanding the tax base, enhancing compliance, and integrating technology in tax administration.

4. Nepal

Before the 1950s:

Nepal had a traditional tax system with little focus on income tax.

Post-1990s:

Post-democratization, Nepal introduced more structured income tax laws, with periodic revisions to align with economic changes.

Recent Developments:

Recent years have seen a shift towards broadening the tax base and revising tax rates, including personal income tax slabs.

5. Haiti

20th Century:

Haiti's tax system was underdeveloped for much of the 20th century, with a heavy reliance on trade taxes.

21st Century:

Efforts have been made to modernize the tax system, though progress is slow due to political instability and economic challenges.

Recent Efforts:

Recent efforts focus on improving tax administration and compliance, with some adjustments in income and corporate tax structures.

These summaries provide a glimpse into the complex evolution of tax systems in developing countries. Each country has unique challenges and solutions based on its economic, political, and social context. The information is broad and may not cover all specific changes, but it offers a general view of the direction in which these countries are moving regarding tax policy and administration.

Now let's have a look at the income tax history and significant periodical changes related to salary and compensation in a few developed countries.

It's important to note that income tax systems in these countries are often complex and have evolved over a long period, influenced by various economic, political, and social factors.

1. United States

Early 20th Century:

The modern federal income tax was established in 1913 with the 16th Amendment. Initially, it applied to only a small percentage of the population.

World War II:

Tax rates increased significantly, and the tax base broadened.

Post-War Period: Introduction of adjustments for inflation, tax brackets, and deductions.

1980s - 1990s:

Major tax reforms under Reagan and Clinton, focusing on simplifying the tax code and adjusting rates.

21st Century:

Continued adjustments, including Bush-era tax cuts, Obama-era tax increases on high earners, and the Trump Administration's Tax Cuts and Jobs Act of 2017.

2. United Kingdom

19th Century:

Modern income tax was reintroduced in 1842 by Sir Robert Peel; it had previously been used in the Napoleonic Wars.

World War II:

Significant increases in tax rates and the number of people taxed.

1970s:

The highest marginal tax rate reached 83%.

1980s:

Major reforms under Margaret Thatcher, including significant rate reductions.

21st Century:

Continued adjustments, focusing on tax bands and allowances, with recent discussions around tax in the digital age.

3. Germany

Early 20th Century:

Income tax was introduced in the early 1920s.

Post-World War II:

The tax system was restructured, with progressive rates and various deductions.

1990s - Reunification:

Tax system adjustments to integrate East and West Germany.

21st Century:

Reforms to reduce tax rates, simplify the tax system, and adjust to EU regulations.

4. Japan

Late 19th Century:

The modern tax system was established in the Meiji period.

Post-World War II:

High progressive tax rates introduced.

1980s - 1990s:

Tax reforms to stimulate economic growth, including rate reductions.

21st Century:

Focus on dealing with the national debt and ageing population, with adjustments in tax rates and social security contributions.

5. Canada

1917:

Introduction of income tax as a temporary measure during World War I, which became permanent.

Post-War Period:

Progressive tax rates with various deductions and credits.

1980s - 1990s:

Tax reforms focusing on rate reductions and base broadening.

21st Century:

Adjustments reflecting economic conditions, including tax cuts and increases, and emphasis on tax benefits for families and low-income individuals.

These histories showcase the evolution of tax systems in response to economic demands, wars, social changes, and political ideologies. Developed countries typically have gone through phases of high taxation, particularly during and after major conflicts, followed by periods of reform and restructuring aimed at stimulating economic growth, ensuring fairness, and adapting to modern challenges.

Income Tax History of India

Here's an overview of the income tax history in India, highlighting key periodical changes and their impacts on salary and compensation:

1. Early History (1860-1947)

1860:

Income tax was first introduced in India by James Wilson to compensate for the losses incurred by the British government during the First War of Independence against British rule.

1870-1947:

Various amendments and modifications were made, but income tax remained a moderate source of government revenue during the British Raj.

2. Post-Independence Era (1947-1960s)

1947:

After independence, the income tax law was inherited from the British.

1960s:

High tax rates for higher income brackets were introduced, reflecting a socialist economic approach.

1961:

The Income Tax Act was enacted, which is the foundational law governing income tax in India today.

3. 1970s-1980s

1970s:

Peak income tax rates were extremely high, at times exceeding 90% for the highest income brackets.

1980s:

Gradual reduction in tax rates began, aimed at encouraging compliance and broadening the tax base.

4. Economic Liberalization (1991 onwards)

1991:

Economic liberalization led to significant reforms in the tax system.

1992-93:

Tax rates were substantially lowered, the number of tax slabs was reduced, and the peak rate was brought down to 40%.

Impact:

This period saw a shift in focus from tax collection from a few at high rates to a larger base at more reasonable rates.

5. 21st Century Reforms

2000s:

Introduction of new tax slabs, with continual adjustments for inflation and economic changes.

2010s:

Further rationalization of tax slabs and rates, including the introduction of new categories like the super-rich tax.

2016:

Demonetization had an indirect impact on income tax, with a focus on increasing the taxpayer base and reducing cash transactions.

2020:

The introduction of a new tax regime with lower tax rates but without exemptions, alongside the existing regime with higher rates and exemptions.

Impact:

These changes aimed to simplify the tax system, encourage voluntary compliance, and make the tax system more progressive.

6. Current Trends and Future Outlook

Digitalization:

Increased focus on digital filing and processing of tax returns.

COVID-19 Relief Measures:

Temporary tax relief measures to alleviate economic stress by the pandemic.

Future Projections:

There is ongoing discussion about further simplifying the tax regime, and possibly moving towards a more streamlined slab system.

Impact of Income Tax on Salary and Compensation

Tax Slabs and Rates:

Changes in tax slabs and rates directly affect the net income of salaried individuals.

Deductions and Exemptions:

Various deductions (like 80C, 80D) and exemptions allowed salaried individuals to reduce taxable income, impacting take-home pay.

Corporate Tax Changes:

Shifts in corporate tax rates also indirectly affect salary structures, as companies adjust compensation based on their tax liabilities and economic conditions.

India's income tax system has evolved from a highly progressive and complex structure with extremely high rates to a more simplified and rationalized system. The focus has increasingly been on widening the tax base, ensuring compliance, and making the system more taxpayer-friendly while adapting to economic and global changes.

How income tax system and other taxes affect salary and compensation.

Explanation with examples of developing and developed countries.

The income tax system and other forms of taxation significantly impact salaries and compensation in both developed and developing countries. These impacts manifest in various ways, influencing the net income of individuals, the financial strategies of businesses, and the overall economic environment.

Below, I have provided examples and explanations to illustrate these effects.

Developed Countries

1. The United States

Progressive Tax System:

The U.S. employs a progressive income tax system, where tax rates increase with higher income brackets. For instance, an individual earning $40,000 a year might pay a federal tax rate of 12%, while someone earning $400,000 might pay 35%.

Impact on Net Income:

Higher earners have a larger portion of their income taxed, which affects their take-home pay. This system aims to be equitable by taxing individuals according to their ability to pay.

Employee Benefits and Tax Deductions:

In the U.S., many employers offer health insurance, retirement savings plans, and other benefits. These benefits are often tax-advantaged, meaning they are either tax-exempt or tax-deferred, making them a crucial part of compensation packages.

2. Germany

High Taxation and Social Security Contributions:

Germany is known for high tax rates and substantial social security contributions. These fund extensive social welfare programs, including healthcare, unemployment benefits, and pensions.

Effect on Salaries:

The high tax burden can reduce net salaries but is offset by the high level of social services provided. This trade-off is generally accepted as part of the social contract in Germany.

Developing Countries

1. India

Moderate to High Taxation with Exemptions:

India has a progressive tax system, but with lower thresholds compared to many developed countries. Tax exemptions for various investments and expenses (like housing loans, insurance, etc.) play a significant role.

Impact on Disposable Income:

For many middle-class individuals, the effective tax rate might be lowered due to various exemptions. However, the scope of public services in return for these taxes is often perceived as limited, affecting public sentiment towards taxation.

2. Brazil

Complex Tax System with Indirect Taxes:

Brazil has a complex tax system with a significant burden of indirect taxes like VAT (Value Added Tax). These indirect taxes can disproportionately affect lower-income individuals.

Salary and Consumption Impact:

The high level of indirect taxation increases the cost of living, which can negate the effects of salary increases, especially for the lower and middle class.

General Effects of Taxation on Salaries and Compensation

1. Disposable Income:

Higher taxes reduce disposable income, affecting consumer spending and saving habits.

2. Cost of Living Adjustments:

In countries with high taxation, salaries often need to be higher to maintain a comparable standard of living.

3. Employee Benefits:

In countries with lower public service provisions, companies might offer more comprehensive benefit packages to attract talent.

4. Incentives for Skill Development:

Tax incentives for education and training can influence individual decisions to pursue further skill development, indirectly affecting their compensation potential.

5. Business Strategies:

Companies in high-tax countries might implement strategies to maximize tax efficiency, influencing how they structure compensation and benefits.

Conclusion

The impact of the income tax system and other forms of taxation on salaries and compensation is multifaceted and varies significantly between developed and developing countries. In developed countries, higher taxes often fund extensive social services, affecting net salaries but providing substantial public benefits. In developing countries, the impact is more varied, with challenges including complex tax systems, indirect taxation affecting the cost of living, and varying levels of public services in return for taxes paid. Understanding these dynamics is crucial for individuals in managing their finances and for policymakers in designing tax systems that balance revenue needs with economic growth and equity.

"Employees who feel fairly compensated are more likely to be engaged, committed, and productive."

Chapter 21

Profit Management for New Ventures

Embark on a transformative journey into the realm of profit management for new ventures. In this chapter, we delve into the strategic intricacies and practical methodologies that underpin effective profit management strategies. From optimizing revenue streams to minimizing costs, we uncover the essential principles and innovative approaches that drive sustainable financial growth. Through insightful analyses and real-world examples, we empower entrepreneurs to navigate the complex terrain of profit management with confidence and foresight. Join us as we unlock the keys to unlocking the full potential of your venture's profitability.

Best ways to manage profits by newly formed organizations and entrepreneurs

Managing profits effectively is crucial for the success and sustainability of newly formed organizations and entrepreneurs. Here are some best practices and methods to manage profits:

1. Financial Planning and Budgeting

Create a Comprehensive Budget:

Develop a detailed budget outlining expected revenues and expenses. Regularly review and update the budget based on actual financial performance.

Allocate Resources Wisely:

Prioritize spending based on essential needs and strategic goals. Allocate resources efficiently to maximize returns.

2. Cost Control and Expense Management

Monitor and Analyze Expenses:

Regularly analyze operational expenses to identify areas for cost savings. Negotiate better deals with suppliers and explore cost-effective alternatives.

Implement Cost Controls:

Set policies and controls to manage discretionary spending. Ensure that expenses align with business priorities.

3. Invest in Growth Opportunities

Strategic Investments:

Identify and invest in opportunities that align with the long-term growth strategy. This could include expanding product lines, entering new markets, or investing in technology.

Evaluate ROI:

Assess the return on investment (ROI) for each expenditure to ensure that it contributes positively to overall profitability.

4. Build and Retain Customer Relationships

Customer Retention Strategies:

Focus on retaining existing customers through excellent service, loyalty programs, and customer engagement. Repeat business is often more cost-effective than acquiring new customers.

Customer Feedback and Innovation:

Use customer feedback to enhance products or services. Innovate based on customer needs to stay competitive and maintain a loyal customer base.

5. Diversification and Risk Management

Diversify Revenue Streams:

Avoid overreliance on a single source of revenue. Diversification can provide stability and mitigate risks associated with changes in the market or industry.

Risk Assessment and Mitigation:

Regularly assess business risks and implement strategies to mitigate them. This includes financial, operational, and market risks.

6. Debt Management and Financing

Prudent Use of Debt:

If leveraging debt, do so prudently. Evaluate the cost of debt and ensure that the returns generated from its use exceed the associated costs.

Explore Financing Options:

Consider various financing options, including equity funding, venture capital, or loans, based on the business's specific needs and growth plans.

7. Employee Productivity and Talent Management

Invest in Employee Development:

Support employee training and development to enhance skills and productivity. Engaged and skilled employees contribute positively to the bottom line.

Performance-Based Compensation:

Align compensation structures with performance to motivate employees and link their success to the company's profitability.

8. Tax Planning and Compliance

Efficient Tax Planning:

Seek professional advice to optimize tax planning. Understand available deductions, credits, and incentives to minimize the tax burden.

Compliance with Tax Regulations:

Ensure compliance with tax laws and regulations to avoid penalties and legal issues.

9. Regular Financial Analysis and Reporting

Financial Reporting:

Establish regular financial reporting practices. Analyze financial statements to gain insights into profitability, cash flow, and key performance indicators.

Key Performance Metrics:

Define and track key performance metrics relevant to the business to measure success and identify areas for improvement.

10. Sustainable Practices and Social Responsibility

Corporate Social Responsibility (CSR):

Integrate sustainable and socially responsible practices. CSR initiatives can enhance brand reputation and contribute to long-term success.

Conclusion

Effective profit management involves a combination of strategic planning, cost control, customer focus, risk management, and talent development. Entrepreneurs and new organizations should adopt a holistic approach, continually reassessing and adapting strategies to navigate the dynamic business landscape. Regularly seeking professional advice and staying informed about industry trends are also key components of successful profit management.

"Compensation should reflect not just the job, but the value and impact of the individual."

Chapter 22

Expense Management for New Ventures

Strategic Expense Management for New Ventures

Embark on a transformative journey into the realm of expense management for new ventures in "Expense Management for New Ventures." In this chapter, we delve into the strategic intricacies and practical methodologies that underpin effective expense management strategies. From optimizing resource allocation to implementing cost-saving measures, we uncover the essential principles and innovative approaches that drive sustainable financial efficiency. Through insightful analyses and real-world examples, we empower entrepreneurs to navigate the complex terrain of expense management with confidence and foresight. Join us as we unlock the keys to optimizing your venture's expenditure for long-term success.

Best ways to manage expenses by newly formed organizations and entrepreneurs

Effectively managing expenses is crucial for the success and sustainability of newly formed organizations and entrepreneurs.

Here are some best practices and strategies to manage expenses efficiently:

1. Create a Detailed Budget

Forecast Revenue and Expenses:

Develop a comprehensive budget outlining expected revenues and expenses. Regularly review and update the budget as business conditions change.

Prioritize Spending:

Identify essential expenses and prioritize spending based on critical business needs.

2. Control Operational Costs

Monitor and Analyze Expenses Regularly:

Regularly review operational expenses to identify areas for cost savings. Leverage technology and automation to streamline processes and reduce operational costs.

Negotiate with Suppliers:

Negotiate favourable terms with suppliers and explore bulk purchasing or long-term contracts to secure discounts.

3. Embrace Cost-Effective Technology

Cloud Solutions and SaaS:

Embrace cloud-based solutions and Software as a Service (SaaS) to reduce the need for expensive hardware and software purchases.

Automation Tools:

Invest in automation tools to streamline repetitive tasks, improving efficiency and reducing labour costs.

4. Remote Work and Flexible Work Arrangements

Remote Work Options:

Consider remote work options to reduce costs associated with office space, utilities, and related expenses.

Flexible Work Hours:

Implement flexible work hours to optimize employee productivity and potentially reduce overhead costs.

5. Outsourcing and Freelancing

Outsource Non-Core Functions:

Consider outsourcing non-core functions to reduce labour costs and gain access to specialized skills without the need for full-time employees.

Freelance Talent:

Utilize freelance talent for specific projects or tasks, providing flexibility without the commitment of permanent employment.

6. Employee Expense Management

Expense Policies:

Establish clear expense policies for employees to ensure responsible spending.

Employee Training:

Train employees on cost-conscious practices and the importance of managing expenses effectively.

7. Energy Efficiency and Sustainability

Energy Conservation:

Implement energy-efficient practices to reduce utility costs. This includes using energy-efficient appliances, optimizing lighting, and adopting sustainable practices.

Sustainable Practices:

Consider environmentally friendly practices that not only contribute to cost savings but also align with corporate social responsibility.

8. Vendor Management

Regularly Review Vendor Contracts:

Periodically review vendor contracts to identify cost-saving opportunities and negotiate better terms.

Explore Alternative Suppliers:

Continuously explore alternative suppliers to ensure competitive pricing.

9. Travel and Entertainment

Virtual Meetings:

Utilize virtual meetings and video conferencing to reduce travel expenses.

Expense Approval Systems:

Implement systems for managing travel and entertainment expenses with clear approval processes.

10. Continuous Improvement and Feedback

Feedback Loops:

Encourage feedback from employees on potential cost-saving ideas. Create a culture of continuous improvement.

Benchmarking:

Regularly benchmark expenses against industry standards to identify areas for improvement.

Conclusion

Effectively managing expenses requires a proactive approach, continuous monitoring, and adaptability to changing business conditions. By implementing these strategies, newly formed organizations and entrepreneurs can optimize their spending, increase operational efficiency, and contribute to the overall financial health of their business. Regularly reassessing and adjusting expense management strategies based on evolving business needs is essential for long-term success.

"Fair pay isn't just a nice-to-have; it's a necessity for morale and productivity."

Chapter 23

Employee Commitments in Supportive Workplace: Responsibilities and Contributions

Welcome to the final chapter of our journey, where we illuminate the pivotal role of employee commitments in fostering supportive workplaces. In "Employee Commitments in a Supportive Workplace: Responsibilities and Contributions," we explore the symbiotic relationship between organizations and their employees. Here, we unravel the core responsibilities and contributions expected from employees within a nurturing work environment. From performance excellence to unwavering dedication, we dissect the key elements that define exemplary employee commitments. Through compelling insights and actionable strategies, we empower organizations to cultivate a culture of mutual respect, trust, and collaboration. Join us as we champion the values of integrity, accountability, and camaraderie, driving sustainable success and fulfilment for both employers and employees alike.

When an organization or company provides adequate care to its employees in terms of salary and compensation, employees typically have several responsibilities in return:

1. Performance Excellence:

Employees are expected to perform their duties with excellence and meet or exceed the expectations set for their roles. This includes completing tasks efficiently, meeting deadlines, and achieving goals or targets.

2. Commitment and Dedication:

Employees should demonstrate commitment and dedication to their work and the organization's objectives. This involves being punctual, reliable and engaged in their tasks, as well as displaying a positive attitude towards their responsibilities.

3. Professionalism:

Employees are expected to maintain a high level of professionalism in their conduct and interactions with colleagues, clients, and stakeholders. This includes adhering to company policies and procedures, as well as maintaining confidentiality and integrity in their work.

4. Continuous Learning and Development:

Employees should proactively seek opportunities for learning and skill development to enhance their professional growth and contribute more effectively to the organization. This may involve participating in training programs, acquiring new certifications, or pursuing further education.

5. Team Collaboration:

Employees are often required to collaborate with colleagues and contribute to a positive team environment. This includes sharing knowledge and expertise, supporting team members when needed, and fostering open communication and cooperation.

6. Adaptability and Flexibility:

In today's dynamic business environment, employees should demonstrate adaptability and flexibility to navigate changes and challenges effectively. This may involve adjusting to new tasks, technologies, or processes, and being open to feedback and constructive criticism.

7. Alignment with Organizational Values:

Employees are expected to align their actions and behaviours with the values and culture of the organization. This includes promoting diversity, equity, and inclusion, as well as upholding ethical standards and corporate social responsibility initiatives.

By fulfilling these responsibilities, employees contribute to the overall success and growth of the organization while fostering a mutually beneficial relationship with their employer.

Conclusion

In conclusion, when organizations prioritize providing adequate care to their employees in terms of salary and compensation, it sets the stage for a reciprocal relationship where employees also have important responsibilities to fulfil. These responsibilities, including performance excellence, commitment, professionalism, continuous learning, team collaboration, adaptability, and alignment with organizational values, form the foundation of a supportive workplace culture. By meeting these expectations, employees not only contribute to the organization's success but also benefit from personal and professional growth opportunities. This symbiotic relationship between employers and employees fosters a positive work environment where mutual respect, trust, and collaboration thrive, ultimately driving organizational excellence and long-term success.

"Aligning compensation with performance incentivizes excellence and drives results."

Chapter 24

FAQs and Troubleshooting

This chapter addresses common and frequently asked questions and concerns about salary systems.

Addressing common questions and concerns about salary systems is crucial for employers and HR professionals. Here are some frequently asked questions and detailed, convincing answers to help clarify these issues:

1. How is my salary determined?

Answer:

Salaries are typically determined based on a combination of factors, including the role's market value, experience, education, skills, and the company's compensation philosophy. We also consider internal equity, ensuring fairness and consistency across similar roles within the organization.

2. Why do people in the same role sometimes earn different salaries?

Answer:

Variations in salary within the same role can occur due to differences in individual performance, experience, tenure, or specific skill sets. Sometimes, market changes can impact new hires' salaries. We strive for fairness and regularly review our compensation structures to maintain equity.

3. How often are salaries reviewed?

Answer:

Salaries are typically reviewed annually. However, this can vary depending on the company's policy. These reviews consider market trends, individual performance, and the financial health of the organization.

4. Can I negotiate my salary?

Answer:

Yes, salary negotiations are a part of the hiring process. We encourage candidates to discuss their compensation expectations. Keep in mind, however, that our offers are based on thorough market research and internal equity, and there might be limitations to our negotiation range.

5. What is the difference between a Raise and a Bonus?

Answer:

A raise is a permanent increase in your base salary, often reflecting your performance or market adjustments. A bonus is typically a one-time payment recognizing exceptional performance or as part of company profit-sharing arrangements.

6. Are salaries confidential?

Answer:

While we respect individual privacy, we don't enforce strict salary confidentiality. However, we advise discretion in discussing compensation to maintain a professional and respectful workplace environment.

7. Why haven't I received a Salary Increase?

Answer:

Salary increases are based on several factors, including individual performance, company performance, and market trends. If you haven't received an increase, we encourage you to discuss your performance and development plans with your manager to understand specific areas for improvement and future opportunities.

8. Does the company/ organization offer cost of living adjustments?

Answer:

Yes, our compensation review process takes into account the cost of living changes, particularly in times of significant inflation or economic shifts. These adjustments aim to ensure that salaries remain competitive and fair.

9. What benefits and perks are included in my compensation package?

Answer:

Besides your base salary, your compensation package includes benefits such as health insurance, retirement plans, paid time off, and possibly bonuses or stock options. Specific benefits vary depending on your role and location.

10. How does the company remain competitive with its salaries?

Answer:

We regularly benchmark our salaries against industry standards and adjust our compensation structures accordingly. This ensures we stay competitive in attracting and retaining top talent.

11. What is the policy on overtime pay?

Answer:

Overtime policies vary depending on your role and the country's labour laws. Generally, non-exempt employees are eligible for overtime pay, while exempt employees are not. Specific details about overtime eligibility are outlined in our employee handbook.

Effective communication about salary systems is key to maintaining transparency and trust within an organization. By addressing these common questions clearly and openly, employers can help ensure that their employees have a solid understanding of how their compensation is determined and managed. This understanding is crucial for maintaining a positive and productive workplace environment.

Troubleshooting:

Troubleshooting common issues in compensation management – Offer guidance on common issues that may arise in compensation management and how to address them. Compensation management involves various processes, and like any system, it can encounter challenges.

Here's guidance on troubleshooting common issues in compensation management and how to address them:

1. Pay Inequities:

Issue:

Pay inequities can arise due to biases, inconsistent practices, or lack of transparency.

Guidance:

Regularly conduct pay equity analyses to identify and address any disparities.

Establish clear criteria for determining compensation, considering factors such as experience, skills, and performance.

Promote transparency in compensation decisions to build trust and reduce perceptions of unfairness.

2. Retention Challenges:

Issue:

Difficulty in retaining top talent can be linked to inadequate compensation strategies.

Guidance:

Regularly review and benchmark salaries to ensure they are competitive in the industry.

Implement retention bonuses or benefits to incentivize key employees to stay.

Engage in open communication about career development opportunities tied to compensation.

3. Poor Performance Management:

Issue:

Compensation tied to performance may be ineffective if performance management processes are weak.

Guidance:

Strengthen performance management systems to provide clear expectations and regular feedback.

Ensure that performance metrics align with organizational goals and are communicated effectively.

Conduct regular performance reviews and tie compensation adjustments to performance outcomes.

4. Market Competitiveness Concerns:

Issue:

Falling behind industry standards in terms of compensation can impact talent acquisition and retention.

Guidance:

Regularly benchmark salaries against industry standards and adjust compensation structures accordingly.

Monitor market trends and make proactive changes to stay competitive.

Communicate the organization's commitment to remaining competitive in the talent market.

5. Budget Constraints:

Issue:

Limited budget resources can restrict the ability to offer competitive compensation.

Guidance:

Prioritize compensation areas that have the most significant impact on employee satisfaction and retention.

Explore creative solutions, such as flexible benefits or non-monetary perks, to enhance the overall compensation package.

Communicate openly about budget constraints while emphasizing the organization's commitment to fair and transparent compensation practices.

6. Ineffective Communication:

Issue:

Poor communication about compensation decisions can lead to confusion and dissatisfaction.

Guidance:

Develop a clear and consistent communication strategy for compensation changes.

Provide regular updates on compensation-related matters, ensuring that employees are well-informed.

Encourage an open-door policy for employees to discuss compensation concerns with HR or management.

7. Lack of Employee Engagement:

Issue:

Disengaged employees may not fully appreciate or understand their compensation packages.

Guidance:

Implement communication strategies to help employees understand the link between performance and compensation.

Foster a culture of recognition to increase overall employee engagement.

Encourage feedback and suggestions from employees regarding the compensation structure.

8. Legal Compliance Challenges:

Issue:

Failure to comply with labour laws or changing regulations can lead to legal issues.

Guidance:

Stay informed about labour laws and regulations related to compensation in the relevant jurisdictions.

Regularly review and update compensation policies to ensure compliance.

Seek legal counsel to address any concerns or changes in legislation affecting compensation.

9. Resistance to Change:

Issue:

Employees may resist changes to compensation structures, especially if they perceive a negative impact.

Guidance:

Communicate the reasons for changes and how they align with organizational goals.

Address concerns proactively, providing a platform for employees to voice their opinions and ask questions.

Highlight the long-term benefits and positive aspects of the changes.

10. Limited Data Analytics:

Issue:

Inadequate use of data analytics may hinder the ability to make informed compensation decisions.

Guidance:

Invest in data analytics tools to gather insights on market trends, employee performance, and compensation benchmarks.

Use analytics to identify potential pay gaps and areas for improvement in compensation practices.

Train HR professionals on utilizing data analytics effectively.

Conclusion

Addressing common issues in compensation management requires a proactive and strategic approach. By continuously monitoring, communicating openly, and adapting compensation strategies, organizations can mitigate challenges and build a compensation system that attracts, retains, and motivates top talent while remaining compliant with legal standards.

"Compensation is more than just numbers; it's a reflection of the organization's values and priorities."

Chapter 25

Final Thought

Dear reader,

As we conclude our exploration into the vast and intricate world of salary systems, I am filled with a profound sense of gratitude and accomplishment. Throughout this journey, we have traversed historical landscapes, dissected complex structures, and unlocked the dynamics that shape the way organizations compensate their most valuable asset – their employees.

From the early barter systems to the sophisticated, technology-driven models of today, we have seen how salary systems are not just a reflection of economic transactions, but a mirror to our societal values, aspirations, and advancements. We ventured through various cultures and countries, understanding how developed, developing, and under-developed nations each have unique challenges and strengths in their compensation frameworks.

We delved deep into the heart of what makes a compensation system effective – fairness, competitiveness, and alignment with organizational goals. By exploring various models – from fixed salaries to performance-based incentives, from traditional benefits to flexible and creative perks – we have seen how the essence of a good salary system lies in its ability to motivate, retain, and attract talent while maintaining organizational viability.

As the landscape of work continues to evolve with remote working, gig economies, and AI advancements, we stand at the cusp of another transformation. Our discussion on the future of salary systems offers a glimpse into a world where compensation may no longer be bound by traditional norms but will be a fluid, adaptive construct, ever-responsive to the changing dynamics of work and society.

In closing, I hope this book serves not just as a repository of information, but as a catalyst for thought and innovation in the field of compensation management. Whether you are a business leader, an HR professional, or an employee striving to understand your worth in the marketplace, may this book guide you in navigating the complex yet fascinating world of salary systems.

Thank you for embarking on this enlightening journey with me!

"Recognizing and rewarding employee contributions through fair compensation is key to fostering a culture of appreciation."

Summary

Unlock the Power of Compensation with **"Pay Pulse: It's all about salary and compensation for economic impacts."** Authored by, Avin Nisarg.

This comprehensive guide is designed for entrepreneurs, newly formed organizations, new business ventures, arising business leaders and HR professionals aiming to optimize their workforce management strategies.

This introductory, informative, and concise book is essential reading for every employee, worker, and labourer worldwide as it addresses their well-being, safety, security, and progress.

Delving beyond mere paychecks, this book explores the multifaceted elements of rewarding talent. From understanding the pay structures and importance of fair compensation in attracting and retaining top talent to navigating legal and ethical considerations, **'Pay Pulse'** offers invaluable insights and actionable advice.

This book speaks about every aspect of salary and compensation management, explore emerging trends, real-world case studies, and future projections to keep you ahead in today's competitive landscape.

With practical insights on employee engagement, fundraising, and expense management, **'Pay Pulse'** becomes your go-to resource for maximizing economic impact.

Whether you're a HR professional or a budding entrepreneur, this book equips you with the tools and knowledge needed to optimize compensation strategies, to build a satisfied and motivated workforce, and to drive organizational success.

Get ready to revolutionize your approach to pay management and unleash the full potential of your workforce!

Avin Nisarg
E-mail – naturalavin@gmail.com

"Competitive compensation isn't just about attracting talent; it's about retaining and motivating them."

www.ingramcontent.com/pod-product-compliance
Ingram Content Group UK Ltd.
Pitfield, Milton Keynes, MK11 3LW, UK
UKHW021405190726
13845UKWH00028B/886

9 789334 038880